Tomorrow's Battlefield

Tomorrow's Battlefield: US Proxy Wars and Secret Ops in Africa

Nick Turse

Dispatch Books

Haymarket Books

Published by
Haymarket Books
P.O. Box 180165,
Chicago, IL 60618
773-583-7884
info@haymarketbooks.org
www.haymarketbooks.org

ISBN: 978-1-60846-463-0

Trade distribution:
In the US through Consortium Book Sales
and Distribution, www.cbsd.com
In the UK, Turnaround Publisher Services, www.turnaround-uk.com
In Canada, Publishers Group Canada, www.pgcbooks.ca
All other countries, Publishers Group Worldwide, www.pgw.com

This book was published with the generous support of the Wallace Action
Fund and Lannan Foundation.

Cover image of US Marines teaching crowd control tactics to troops from
Senegal, Burkina Faso, Guinea, and Gambia by Sgt. Tatum Vayavananda.

Printed in Canada by union labor.

Library of Congress CIP Data is available.

1 3 5 7 9 10 8 6 4 2

Table of Contents

Introduction

Tomorrow's Battlefield

On July 12, 2013, as the shrill whistle of a boatswain's call sounded, a cadre of officers from elite military units assembled in a bare-bones building at a US military base in Boeblingen, Germany. On a stage, in front of a humongous American flag, Captain Robert Smith, commanding officer of Naval Special Warfare Group Two; Captain J. Dane Thorleifson, outgoing commander of Naval Special Warfare Unit Ten; and Captain Jay Richards, his successor, took part in a time-honored naval tradition: the change of command ceremony. Before a small crowd of uniformed military personnel and a few civilians, these men, all members of Special Operations Command Africa (SOCAFRICA), spoke about something rarely mentioned in public: covert US military missions in Africa.

By the summer of 2013, representatives of U.S. Africa Command (AFRICOM), the newest of the Defense Department's six geographic combatant commands and the umbrella organization

1

for operations on the continent, had told me again and again that the US military presence there was small, circumscribed, episodic, and, above all, benign. Nothing much of note, they insisted, was going on in Africa. At this closed-door ceremony, before a select crowd of insiders, the officers—whose units include elite Navy SEALs and others expert in counterterrorism missions and capable of launching raids from ships, submarines, and aircraft—offered a very different picture of military operations.

"The mission of Naval Special Warfare Unit Ten does not pause," Smith told the audience. "Forces are deploying, as we speak, down on the African continent. Forces are already staged on the African continent executing the Naval Special Warfare Unit Ten mission, the SOCAFRICA mission, and the AFRICOM mission. That mission does not stop." He added, "Some people like to think that Africa is our next ridgeline," and then set his audience straight. "Africa is our current ridgeline."

Smith also described partnerships with African militaries across the continent, from Uganda to Somalia to Nigeria, while lauding departing commander Thorleifson's efforts: "He has led this fight with his own boots on the ground in Africa." That caught my attention. It sure didn't sound like the standard AFRICOM line about a "small footprint" on the continent, mostly involving humanitarian operations. It sounded as if he was saying that America was already at war in Africa.

Smith presented Thorleifson with the Legion of Merit, in part for creating a strategy for "persistent engagements in five Special Operations Command Africa priority countries." Then Thorleifson took to the lectern himself and offered an even more striking vision of US operations.

Reflecting on two years spent commanding Naval Special Warfare Unit Ten, he discussed the "high tempo" of operations, with personnel "deployed 365 days a year in over half a dozen disparate, austere locations" and lauded his troops for successfully operating in a "complex battlespace." Then he quoted his boss, then Brigadier (now Major) General James Linder, the commander of US Special Operations forces in Africa, looking on from the audience. "General Linder has been saying, 'Africa is the battlefield of tomorrow, today.' And, sir, I couldn't agree more. This new battlefield is custom made for SOC and we'll thrive in it. It's exactly where we need to be today and I expect we'll be for some time in the future."

My ears perked up. The commander of a shadowy quick-reaction force agreeing with his commander, the chief of the most elite American troops in Africa, that the continent wasn't a sleepy backwater, as AFRICOM's spokespeople and public affairs personnel claimed; it wasn't even the war zone of tomorrow. It was today's battlefield. This hush-hush ceremony corroborated exactly what my own reporting had uncovered over the previous year and convinced me that I needed to keep digging into just what the U.S. military was doing—far from prying eyes—on the African continent.

The Great AFRICOM Runaround

The path that led me to this point was, like so many others in life, winding and unexpected. For years, as I investigated other wars elsewhere on the planet, I half-noticed stories about US military activities in Africa but paid them no serious attention. I did a little digging once or twice, but nothing came of it. In 2005, I wrote a short chapter on US military missions in Africa for my first book, but it ended up on the cutting-room floor. At one point, the military even offered me an opportunity to visit its lone avowed base on the continent, Camp Lemonnier in the tiny Horn of Africa nation of Djibouti, but I had no media outlet interested in paying my way and so never went.

In 2010, with the Iraq War winding down and a presidential promise that the same would eventually happen in Afghanistan, I began to note mounting evidence of increasingly robust US military activity in Africa. By the next year, I was sure something big was happening, so I took the idea to my boss at a news website where I had just been made a senior editor. Sitting in a chain eatery in New York City, I pitched the idea of a big investigative piece on shadowy US military operations in Africa. His face said it all—and then so did his mouth. Nobody is interested in Africa, readers won't care, and he didn't want me wasting time on a deep-dive investigation into a hopeless nonstory. I got the message loud and clear. Luckily Tom Engelhardt, my editor and colleague at TomDispatch.com, had the exact opposite reaction to my pitch and encouraged me to get started.

By the time I cleared out other projects and set to work, it was 2012 and, on July 12—exactly one year to the day before the change of command ceremony in Boeblingen and following a considerable amount of investigation of open-source material and little-noticed military documents—I published "Obama's Scramble for Africa: Secret Wars, Secret Bases, and the Pentagon's 'New Spice Route,'" now the first chapter of this book. More than two years later, I'm still at it, still digging into US. military missions in Africa, sifting through formerly classified documents and restricted reports and, on occasion, reporting from the continent.

I never intended to make Africa my beat. That initial article could easily have been a one-off piece and I might have returned to coverage of the US war in Afghanistan or global drone operations or begun researching US military missions in South America or something else entirely. What spurred me to stick with Africa were the reactions of US Africa Command.

When I posed questions to an AFRICOM spokesman for that first article, I felt like I was being spun. What he was telling me just didn't jibe with what I was discovering through my research. Instead of responses that seemed genuine, I heard talking points that were clearly canned, not candor. It raised my suspicions. Later, when I asked to visit US. facilities to see things for myself, I was turned down. When I sought interviews with commanders, it was the same drill. It seemed like AFRICOM had something to hide.

About a week after that first piece of mine was published, TomDispatch received a "letter to the editor" from Colonel Tom Davis, director of US Africa Command's Office of Public Affairs, disputing in some detail a number of my contentions and calling attention to numerous perceived inaccuracies. On top of that, he sent a copy of the letter to the head of the Nation Institute, the nonprofit media center that supports TomDispatch.

At 2,500 carefully parsed words, it was clear that AFRICOM had put significant time and effort into an attempt to undermine the credibility of my piece. I also took their copying of the letter to the Nation Institute as an attempt at intimidation and an effort to tarnish my reporting in the eyes of TomDispatch's parent organization and funder. I was instantly energized and—with Engelhardt's and the Nation Institute's full support and backing—raring to respond. I did so a few days later in a "debate" at TomDispatch in which we published Davis's letter and my detailed reply, both included in an appendix to this volume. Basically, our dispute boiled down to my contention that the United States had an expanding presence in Africa, marked by an increase in operations and outposts, and Davis's assertions that the presence was insignificant and so hardly worth mentioning.

When the dust settled, I personally wrote to Davis and asked him for, among other information, a full listing of what he called "temporary facilities," as well as all bases, camps, supply depots, and other sites that might be used by US personnel in Africa in an effort to gauge the full scope of the American presence on the continent. Four days later, AFRICOM spokesman Eric Elliott emailed to say Davis was on leave, but added, "Let me see what I can give you in response to your request for a complete list of facilities. There will [be] some limits on the details we can provide because of the scope of the request."

Were there ever!

That was August 2012. For months, I heard nothing. Not an apology for the wait, not a request for more time. A follow-up in late October was ignored. A note in early November was finally answered by still another AFRICOM spokesman, Lieutenant Commander Dave Hecht, who said he was now on the case and would get back to me with an update by the end of the week. You won't be shocked to learn that the weekend came and went without a word. I sent another follow-up. On November 16, Hecht finally responded: "All questions now have answers. I just need the boss to review before I can release. I hope to have them to you by mid next week."

Take a guess what happened next. Nada. Further emails went unanswered. It was December before Hecht replied: "All questions have been answered but are still being reviewed for release. Hopefully this week I can send everything your way."

He didn't.

In January 2013, answers to some other questions of mine finally arrived, but nothing on my request for information on US bases. By now, Hecht, too, had disappeared and I was passed off to AFRICOM's chief of media engagement, Benjamin Benson.

When I asked about the ignored questions, he responded that my request "exceed[ed] the scope of this command's activities, and of what we are resourced to research and provide under the Public Affairs program." I should instead, he suggested, file a request under the Freedom of Information Act. In other words, I should begin what was guaranteed to be another endlessly drawn-out process. (Still, I did exactly that. And almost two years later, I continue to wait for those documents.)

I was, shall we say, irritated. Somehow, it had taken six months to get me nothing and send me elsewhere. I said as much to Benson. He wrote back: "Lastly, you state, 'I've been led astray for the better part of a year and intend to write about it,' which of course is your right to do in our free society. We expect that as a professional, you convey the correct facts, and ask that you note that we did research, and provide answers to the questions you posed."

Duly noted, Ben. Or at least let me note that you sent me next to nothing and I set to work figuring it out myself.

When we next spoke by telephone, weeks after his email, I reiterated that I understood he couldn't offer me a list of the locations of US bases in Africa due to "security of operations," so all I now wanted was a simple count of facilities in Africa. "That's tricky. We have teams coming in and out of Africa to different locations all the time," he replied. "Places that they might be, the range of possible locations can get really big, but can provide a really skewed image of where we are . . . versus other places where we have ongoing operations. So, in terms of providing number, I'd be at a loss of how to quantify this."

It seemed easy enough to me: just count them and include the necessary disclaimers. So I asked if AFRICOM kept a count of where its troops were located. They did. So what was the problem? He launched into a monologue about the difficulty of ascertaining just what truly constituted "a location" and then told me: "We don't have a way that we really count locations."

It couldn't have been clearer by then. They had a count of all locations, but couldn't count them. They had lists of where all US troops in Africa were based, but not a list of bases. It was a classic runaround, and it caught perfectly the nature of my dealings with the command over these last years.

At every turn, AFRICOM and its subordinate units have put genuine effort into thwarting my reporting efforts—from ignoring requests for basic information to agreeing to and then abruptly canceling interviews. While journalists from newspapers and magazines that tell AFRICOM-friendly stories are offered access to top officers, hush-hush outposts, and firsthand looks at training exercises, my requests for similar access have regularly and repeatedly been denied or ignored.

As a result, I've had to be more creative. That means paying attention to largely unnoticed public documents, filing Freedom of Information Act requests, taking a firsthand look at US "success" stories in Africa to see if they resemble reality, and keeping an eye out for what AFRICOM officers say when they're not spouting the party line—like when they speak to each other at a change-of-command ceremony on a military base in Germany.

Their Pivot and Mine

While America's "pivot" to Africa began during the George W. Bush years, it has grown enormously under President Barack Obama—with missions across the continent jumping by more than 200 percent during his tenure. Airstrikes and commando raids in Libya, black ops missions and drone assassinations in Somalia, a proxy war in Mali, shadowy ops in Chad, antipiracy efforts in the Gulf of Guinea. The list goes on and on.

The Pentagon's pivot to Africa has been mirrored by my own. What follows are the results of that pivot, a look at a war zone spanning almost fifty countries that you weren't meant to know about, a war zone the size of the United States, China, India, and most of Europe combined, a war zone that doesn't officially exist because, outside of commanders' conclaves and briefings for defense contractors, the American military claims it's not at war in Africa. But the evidence of that war and early signs of its failure are out there—from a remote drone base in Niger to a crumbling hearts-and-minds project in Djibouti, from ill-fated schemes to train Libyan militiamen to a Christmas-in-July party at the US embassy in South Sudan.

So much remains secret, unreported, buried in Pentagon files, known only to Navy SEALs and Army Green Berets, shadowy private contractors, and tight-lipped AFRICOM commanders, but I've done my best to sketch in the broad outlines of the US military's move into Africa and fill in some of the gaps, to shed light on missions that were long in the dark, and suggest where we might be headed in the months and years ahead. You're about to take a tour of a war zone few people know about, of secret ops and secret bases, a tour of tomorrow's battlefield, today.

Nick Turse
March 2015

1

America's Shadow Wars in Africa: Obama's Scramble for Africa

July 12, 2012

They call it the New Spice Route, an homage to the medieval trade network that connected Europe, Africa, and Asia, even if today's "spice road" has nothing to do with cinnamon, cloves, or silks. Instead, it's a superpower's superhighway, on which trucks and ships shuttle fuel, food, and military equipment through a growing maritime and ground transportation infrastructure to a network of supply depots, tiny camps, and airfields meant to service a fast-growing US military presence in Africa.

Few in the United States know about this superhighway, or about the dozens of training missions and joint military exercises being carried out in nations that most Americans couldn't locate on a map. Even fewer have any idea that military officials are invoking the names of Marco Polo and the queen of Sheba as they build a bigger military footprint in Africa. It's all happening in the shadows of what in a previous imperial age was known as "the Dark Continent."

In East African ports, huge metal shipping containers arrive with the everyday necessities for a military on the make. They're then loaded onto trucks that set off down rutted roads toward dusty bases and distant outposts.

On the highway from Djibouti to Ethiopia, for example, one can see the bare outlines of this shadow war at the truck stops where local drivers take a break from their long-haul routes. The same is true in other African countries. The nodes of the network tell part of the story: Manda Bay, Garissa, and Mombasa in Kenya; Kampala and Entebbe in Uganda; Bangui and Djema in the Central African Republic; Nzara in South Sudan; Dire Dawa in Ethiopia; and the Pentagon's showpiece African base, Camp Lemonnier, in Djibouti, among others.

According to Pat Barnes, a spokesman for US Africa Command (AFRICOM), Camp Lemonnier serves as the only official U.S. base on the continent. "There are more than 2,000 U.S. personnel stationed there," he told TomDispatch by email. "The primary AFRICOM organization at Camp Lemonnier is Combined Joint Task Force-Horn of Africa (CJTF-HOA). CJTF-HOA's efforts are focused in East Africa and they work with partner nations to assist them in strengthening their defense capabilities."

Barnes also noted that Department of Defense personnel are assigned to US embassies across Africa, including twenty-one individual Offices of Security Cooperation responsible for facilitating military-to-military activities with "partner nations." He characterized the forces involved as small teams carrying out pinpoint missions. Barnes did admit that in "several locations in Africa, AFRICOM has a small and temporary presence of personnel. In all cases, these military personnel are guests within host-nation facilities, and work alongside or coordinate with host-nation personnel."

Shadow Wars

In 2003, when CJTF-HOA was first set up there, it was indeed true that the only major US outpost in Africa was Camp Lemonnier. In the ensuing years, in quiet and largely unnoticed ways, the Pentagon and the CIA have been spreading their forces across the continent. Today—official designations aside—the United States maintains a surprising number of bases in Africa. And "strengthening" African armies turns out to be a truly elastic rubric for what's going on.

Under President Obama, in fact, operations in Africa have accelerated far beyond the more limited interventions of the Bush years: the 2011 war in Libya; a regional drone campaign with missions run out of airports and bases in Djibouti, Ethiopia, and the Indian Ocean archipelago nation of Seychelles; a flotilla of thirty ships in that ocean supporting regional operations; a multi-pronged military and CIA campaign against militants in Somalia, including intelligence operations, training for Somali agents, a secret prison, helicopter attacks, and US commando raids; a massive influx of cash for counterterrorism operations across East Africa; a possible old-fashioned air war, carried out on the sly in the region using manned aircraft; tens of millions of dollars in arms for allied mercenaries and African troops; and a special ops expeditionary force (bolstered by State Department experts) dispatched to help capture or kill Lord's Resistance Army leader Joseph Kony and his senior commanders. And this only begins to scratch the surface of Washington's fast-expanding plans and activities in the region.

To support these mushrooming missions, near-constant training operations, and alliance-building joint exercises, outposts of all sorts are sprouting continent-wide, connected by a sprawling shadow logistics network. Most American bases in Africa are still small and austere, but growing ever larger and more permanent in appearance. For example, photographs from 2011 of Ethiopia's Camp Gilbert, examined by TomDispatch, show a base filled with air-conditioned tents, metal shipping containers, fifty-five-gallon drums, and other gear strapped to pallets, but also recreation facilities with TVs and videogames and a well-appointed gym filled with stationary bikes, free weights, and other equipment.

Continental Drift

After 9/11, the US military moved into three major regions in significant ways: South Asia (primarily Afghanistan), the Middle East (primarily Iraq), and the Horn of Africa. The United States is drawing down in Afghanistan and has left Iraq. Africa, however, remains a growth opportunity for the Pentagon.

The United States is now involved, directly and by proxy, in military and surveillance operations against an expanding list of regional enemies. They include al-Qaeda in the Islamic Maghreb in North Africa; the Islamist movement Boko Haram in Nigeria; al-Qaeda-linked militants in post-Qaddafi Libya; Kony's murderous Lord's Resistance Army (LRA) in the Central African Republic, Congo, and South Sudan; Mali's Islamist Rebels of the Ansar al-Dine, al-Shabaab in Somalia; and guerrillas from al-Qaeda in the Arabian Peninsula across the Gulf of Aden in Yemen.

An investigation by the *Washington Post* revealed that contractor-operated surveillance aircraft based out of Entebbe, Uganda, are scouring the territory used by Kony's LRA at the

Pentagon's behest, and that one hundred to two hundred US commandos share a base with the Kenyan military at Manda Bay. Additionally, US drones are being flown out of Arba Minch airport in Ethiopia and from the Seychelles Islands in the Indian Ocean, while drones and F-15 fighter-bombers have been operating out of Camp Lemonnier as part of the shadow wars being waged by the US military and the CIA in Yemen and Somalia. Surveillance planes used for spy missions over Mali, Mauritania, and the Sahara Desert are also flying missions from Ouagadougou in Burkina Faso, and plans are reportedly in the works for a similar base in the newborn nation of South Sudan.

US Special Operations forces are stationed at a string of even more shadowy forward operating posts on the continent, including one in Djema in the Central Africa Republic and others in Nzara in South Sudan and Dungu in the Democratic Republic of Congo. The United States also has had troops deployed in Mali, despite having officially suspended military relations with that country following a coup.

In addition, according to research by TomDispatch, the US Navy has a forward operating location, manned mostly by Seabees, Civil Affairs personnel, and force-protection troops, known as Camp Gilbert in Dire Dawa, Ethiopia. As well as Camp Lemonnier, the US military also maintains another hole-and-corner outpost in Djibouti, a navy port facility that lacks even a name. AFRICOM did not respond to requests for further information on these posts.

Additionally, US Special Operations forces are engaged in missions against the LRA from a rugged camp in Obo in the Central African Republic, but little is said about that base either. "US military personnel working with regional militaries in the hunt for Joseph Kony are guests of the African security forces comprising the regional counter-LRA effort," Barnes told me. "Specifically in Obo, the troops live in a small camp and work with partner nation troops at a Ugandan facility that operates at the invitation of the government of the Central African Republic."

That's still just part of the story. U.S. troops are also working at sites inside Uganda. Early in 2012, marines from the Special Purpose Marine Air Ground Task Force 12 (SPMAGTF-12) trained soldiers from the Uganda People's Defense Force, which not only runs missions in the Central African Republic but also acts as a proxy force for the United States in Somalia in the battle against the Islamist militants known as al-Shabaab. They now supply the majority of the troops to the African Union Mission protecting the U.S.-supported government in the Somali capital, Mogadishu.

In the spring of 2012, marines from SPMAGTF-12 also trained soldiers from the Burundi National Defense Force (BNDF), the second-largest contingent in Somalia. In the first half of that year, members of Task Force Raptor, 3rd Squadron, 124th Cavalry Regiment, of the Texas National Guard took part in a training mission with the BNDF in Mudubugu, Burundi; SPMAGTF-12 sent trainers to Djibouti to work with an elite local army unit, while other marines traveled to Liberia to focus on teaching riot-control techniques to Liberia's military as part of a State Department–directed effort to rebuild that force.

In addition, the United States conducted counterterrorism training and equipped militaries in Algeria, Burkina Faso, Chad, Mauritania, Niger, and Tunisia. AFRICOM also had fourteen major joint-training exercises in 2012, including missions in Morocco, Cameroon, Gabon, Botswana, South Africa, Lesotho, Senegal, and Nigeria.

The size of US forces conducting these joint exercises and training missions fluctuates, but Barnes told me that, "on an average basis, there are approximately 5,000 US Military and DoD personnel working across the continent" at any one time.

Air Africa

In 2012, the *Washington Post* revealed that since at least 2009, the "practice of hiring private companies to spy on huge expanses of African territory . . . has been a cornerstone of the US military's secret activities on the continent." Dubbed Tusker Sand, the operation consists of contractors flying from Entebbe airport in Uganda and a handful of other airfields. They pilot turbo-prop planes that look innocuous but are packed with sophisticated surveillance gear.

America's mercenary spies in Africa are, however, just part of the story.

While the Pentagon canceled an analogous drone surveillance program dubbed Tusker Wing, it has spent millions of dollars to upgrade the civilian airport at Arba Minch, Ethiopia, to enable drone missions to be flown from it. Infrastructure to support such operations has been relatively cheap and easy to construct, but a much more daunting problem looms—one intimately connected to the New Spice Route.

"Marco Polo wasn't just an explorer," army planner Chris Zahner explained at a conference in Djibouti in 2013. "He was also a logistician developing logistics nodes along the Silk Road. Now let's do something similar where the queen of Sheba traveled." Paeans to bygone luminaries aside, the reasons for pouring resources into sea and ground supply networks have less to do with history than with Africa's airport infrastructure.

Of the 3,300 airfields on the continent identified in a National Geospatial-Intelligence Agency review, the air force has surveyed only 303 of them and just 158 of those surveys are current. Of those airfields that have been checked out, half won't support the weight of the C-130 cargo planes that the US military leans heavily on to transport troops and matériel. These limitations were driven home during Natural Fire 2010, one of that year's joint training exercises hosted by AFRICOM. When C-130s were unable to use an airfield in Gulu, Uganda, an extra $3 million was spent to send in Chinook helicopters.

In addition, diplomatic clearances and airfield restrictions on military aircraft cost the Pentagon time and money, while often raising local suspicion. In an article in the military trade publication *Army Sustainment*, Air Force major Joseph Gaddis touts an emerging solution: outsourcing. The concept was tested during another AFRICOM training operation, Atlas Drop 2011.

"Instead of using military airlift to move equipment to and from the exercise, planners used commercial freight vendors," writes Gadddis. "This provided exercise participants with door-to-door delivery service and eliminated the need for extra personnel to channel the equipment through freight and customs areas." Using mercenary cargo carriers to skirt diplomatic clearance issues and move cargo to airports that can't support C-130s is, however, just one avenue the Pentagon is pursuing to support its expanding operations in Africa.

Another is construction.

The Great Buildup

Military contracting documents reveal plans for an investment of up to $180 million or more in construction at Camp Lemonnier alone. Chief among the projects will be the laying of 54,500 square meters of taxiways "to support medium-load aircraft" and the construction of a 185,000-square-meter Combat Aircraft Loading Area. In addition, plans are in the works to erect modular maintenance structures, hangars, and ammunition storage facilities, all needed for an expanding set of U.S. operations in Africa.

Other contracting documents suggest that in the years to come, the Pentagon will be investing up to $50 million in new projects at that base as well as Kenya's Camp Simba and additional unspecified locations. Still other solicitation materials suggest future military construction in Egypt, where the Pentagon already maintains a medical research facility, and still more work in Djibouti.

No less telling are contracting documents indicating a coming influx of "emergency troop housing" at Camp Lemonnier, including almost three hundred additional containerized living units (CLUs), stackable, air-conditioned living quarters, as well as latrines and laundry facilities.

Military documents also indicate that a nearly $450,000 exercise facility was installed at the US base in Entebbe in 2011. All of this indicates that, for the Pentagon, its African buildup has only begun.

The Scramble for Africa

In a speech in Arlington, Virginia, AFRICOM Commander General Carter Ham explained the reasoning behind US operations on the continent: "The absolute imperative for the United States military [is] to protect America, Americans, and American interests; in our case, in my case, [to] protect us from threats that may emerge from the African continent." As an example, Ham named the Somali-based al-Shabaab as a prime threat. "Why do we care about that?" he asked rhetorically. "Well, al-Qaeda is a global enterprise . . . we think they very clearly do present, as an al-Qaeda affiliate . . . a threat to America and Americans."

Fighting *them* over there, so we don't need to fight *them* here has been a core tenet of American foreign policy for decades, especially since 9/11. But trying to apply military solutions to complex political and social problems has regularly led to unforeseen consequences. For example, the US-supported war in Libya resulted in Tuareg mercenaries, who had been fighting for Libyan autocrat Muammar Qaddafi, heading back to Mali where they helped destabilize that country. The result: a military coup by an American-trained officer; a takeover of some areas by Tuareg fighters of the National Movement for the Liberation of Azawad, who had previously raided Libyan arms depots; and other parts of the country being seized by the irregulars of Ansar al-Dine, the latest al-Qaeda "affiliate" on the American radar. One military intervention, in other words, led to three major instances of blowback in a neighboring country in just a year.

With the Obama administration clearly engaged in a twenty-first-century scramble for Africa, the possibility of successive waves of overlapping blowback grows exponentially. Mali may only be the beginning and there's no telling how any of it will end. In the meantime, keep your eye on Africa. The US military is going to make news there for years to come.

2

Blowback Central:
The Terror Diaspora

June 18, 2013

The Gulf of Guinea. He said it without a hint of irony or embarrassment. This was one of US Africa Command's big success stories. The Gulf . . . of Guinea.

Never mind that most Americans couldn't find it on a map and haven't heard of the nations on its shores like Gabon, Benin, and Togo. Never mind that just five days before I talked with AFRICOM's chief spokesman, the *Economist* had asked if the Gulf of Guinea was on the verge of becoming "another Somalia," because piracy there had jumped 41 percent from 2011 to 2012 and was on track to be even worse in 2013.

The Gulf of Guinea was one of the primary areas in Africa where "stability," the command spokesman assured me, had "improved significantly," and the US military had played a major role in bringing it about. But what did that say about so many other areas of the continent that, since AFRICOM was set up, had been wracked by coups, insurgencies, violence, and volatility?

A careful examination of the security situation in Africa suggests that it is in the process of becoming ground zero for a veritable terror diaspora set in motion in the wake of 9/11 that has only accelerated in the Obama years. Recent history indicates that as US "stability" operations in Africa have increased, militancy has spread, insurgent groups have proliferated, allies have faltered or committed abuses, terrorism has increased, the number of failed states has risen, and the continent has become more unsettled.

The signal event in this tsunami of blowback was the US participation in a war to fell Libyan autocrat Muammar Qaddafi that helped send neighboring Mali, a US-supported bulwark against regional terrorism, into a downward spiral, prompting the intervention of the French military with US backing. The situation could still worsen as the US armed forces grow ever more involved. They are already expanding air operations across the continent, engaging in spy missions for the French military, and using other previously undisclosed sites in Africa.

The Terror Diaspora

In 2000, a report prepared under the auspices of the US Army War College's Strategic Studies Institute examined the "African security environment." While it touched on "internal separatist or rebel movements" in "weak states," as well as nonstate actors like militias and "warlord armies," it made no mention of Islamic extremism or major transnational terrorist threats. In fact, prior to 2001, the United States did not recognize any terrorist organizations in sub-Saharan Africa.

Shortly after the 9/11 attacks, a senior Pentagon official claimed that the US invasion of Afghanistan might drive "terrorists" out of that country and into African nations. "Terrorists associated with al-Qaeda and indigenous terrorist groups have been and continue to be a presence in this region," he said. "These terrorists will, of course, threaten US personnel and facilities."

When pressed about actual transnational dangers, the official pointed to Somali militants but eventually admitted that even the most extreme Islamists there "really have not engaged in acts of terrorism outside Somalia." Similarly, when questioned about connections between Osama bin Laden's core al-Qaeda group and African extremists, he offered only the most tenuous links, like bin Laden's "salute" to Somali militants who killed US troops during the infamous 1993 Black Hawk Down incident.

Despite this, the United States dispatched personnel to Africa as part of Combined Joint Task Force–Horn of Africa in 2002. The next year, CJTF-HOA took up residence at Camp Lemonnier in Djibouti, where it resides to this day on the only officially avowed US base in Africa.

As it was starting up, the State Department launched a multi-million-dollar counterterrorism program, known as the Pan-Sahel Initiative, to bolster the militaries of Mali, Niger, Chad, and Mauritania. In 2004, for example, special forces training teams were sent to Mali as part of the effort. In 2005, the program expanded to include Nigeria, Senegal, Morocco, Algeria, and Tunisia and was renamed the Trans-Saharan Counterterrorism Partnership.

Writing in the *New York Times Magazine*, Nicholas Schmidle noted that the program saw year-round deployments of special forces personnel "to train local armies at battling insurgencies and rebellions and to prevent bin Laden and his allies from expanding into the region." The Trans-Saharan Counterterrorism

Partnership and its Defense Department companion program, then known as Operation Enduring Freedom–Trans-Sahara, were in turn folded into US Africa Command when it took over military responsibility for the continent in 2008.

As Schmidle noted, results in the region seemed at odds with AFRICOM's stated goals. "Al Qaeda established sanctuaries in the Sahel, and in 2006 it acquired a North African franchise [al-Qaeda in the Islamic Maghreb]," he wrote. "Terrorist attacks in the region increased in both number and lethality."

In fact, a look at the official State Department list of terrorist organizations indicates a steady increase in radical Islamic groups in Africa alongside the growth of US counterterrorism efforts there—with the addition of the Libyan Islamic Fighting Group in 2004, Somalia's al-Shabaab in 2008, and Mali's Ansar al-Dine in 2013. In 2012, General Carter Ham, then AFRICOM's chief, added the Islamist militants of Boko Haram in Nigeria to his own list of extremist threats.

The overthrow of Qaddafi in Libya by an interventionist coalition including the United States, France, and Britain similarly empowered a host of new militant Islamist groups such as the Omar Abdul Rahman Brigades, which have since carried out multiple attacks on Western interests, and the al-Qaeda-linked Ansar al-Sharia, whose fighters assaulted US facilities in Benghazi, Libya, on September 11, 2012, killing Ambassador J. Christopher Stevens and three other Americans. In fact, just prior to that attack, according to the *New York Times*, the CIA was tracking "an array of armed militant groups in and around" that one city alone.

According to Frederic Wehrey, a senior policy analyst with the Carnegie Endowment for International Peace and an expert on Libya, that country is now "fertile ground" for militants arriving from the Arabian Peninsula and other places in the Middle East as well as elsewhere in Africa to recruit fighters, receive training, and recuperate. "It's really become a new hub," he told me.

Mission Creep

The US-backed war in Libya and the CIA's efforts in its aftermath are just two of the many operations that have proliferated across the continent under President Barack Obama. These include a multi-pronged military and CIA campaign against militants in Somalia; a special ops expeditionary force (bolstered by State Department experts) dispatched to help capture or kill Lord's Resistance Army leader Joseph Kony and his top lieutenants in the jungles in and around the Central African Republic; a massive influx of funding for counterterrorism operations across East Africa; and, in just the last four years, hundreds of millions of dollars spent arming and training West African troops to serve as American proxies on the continent. From 2010 to 2012, AFRICOM itself burned through $836 million as it expanded its reach across the region, primarily via programs to mentor, advise, and tutor African militaries.

In recent years, the United States has trained and outfitted soldiers from Uganda, Burundi, and Kenya, among other nations, for missions like the hunt for Kony. They have also served as a proxy force for the United States in Somalia, part of the African Union Mission (AMISOM) protecting the US-supported government in that country's capital, Mogadishu. Since 2007, the State Department has anted up about $650 million in logistics support, equipment, and training for AMISOM troops. The Pentagon has kicked in an extra $100 million since 2011.

The United States also continues funding African armies through the Trans-Sahara Counter-Terrorism Partnership and its

Pentagon analog, now known as Operation Juniper Shield, with increased support flowing to Mauritania and Niger in the wake of Mali's collapse. In 2012, the State Department and the US Agency for International Development poured approximately $52 million into the programs, while the Pentagon chipped in another $46 million.

In addition, the Pentagon has run a regional air campaign using drones and manned aircraft out of airports and bases across the continent including Camp Lemonnier, Arba Minch airport in Ethiopia, Niamey in Niger, and the Seychelles Islands in the Indian Ocean, while private contractor–operated surveillance aircraft have flown missions out of Entebbe, Uganda. *Foreign Policy* also reported on the existence of a possible drone base in Lamu, Kenya.

Another critical location is Ouagadougou, the capital of Burkina Faso, home to a Joint Special Operations Air Detachment and the Trans-Sahara Short Take-Off and Landing Airlift Support initiative that, according to military documents, provides for "high-risk activities" carried out by elite forces from Joint Special Operations Task Force-Trans Sahara. Lieutenant Colonel Scott Rawlinson, a spokesman for Special Operations Command Africa, told me that the initiative offers "emergency casualty evacuation support to small team engagements with partner nations throughout the Sahel," although official documents note that such actions have historically accounted for just 10 percent of monthly flight hours.

While Rawlinson demurred from discussing the scope of the program, citing operational security concerns, military documents indicate that it is expanding rapidly. Between March and December 2012, for example, the initiative flew 233 sorties. In just the first three months of 2013, it carried out 193.

AFRICOM spokesman Benjamin Benson has confirmed to TomDispatch that US air operations conducted from Base Aerienne 101 in Niamey, the capital of Niger, were providing "support for intelligence collection with French forces conducting operations in Mali and with other partners in the region." Refusing to go into detail about mission specifics for reasons of "operational security," he added that "in partnership with Niger and other countries in the region, we are committed to supporting our allies . . . this decision allows for intelligence, surveillance, and reconnaissance operations within the region."

Benson was even more tight-lipped about air operations from Nzara Landing Zone in South Sudan, the site of one of several shadowy forward operating posts (including another in Djema in the Central Africa Republic and a third in Dungu in the Democratic Republic of Congo) that have been used by US Special Operations forces. "We don't want Kony and his folks to know . . . what kind of planes to look out for," he said. It's no secret, however, that US air assets over Africa and its coastal waters include Predator, Global Hawk, and Scan Eagle drones; MQ-8 unmanned helicopters; EP-3 Orion aircraft; Pilatus planes; and E-8 Joint Stars aircraft.

In 2012, in its ever-expanding operations, AFRICOM planned fourteen major joint training exercises on the continent, including in Morocco, Uganda, Botswana, Lesotho, Senegal, and Nigeria. One of them, an annual event known as Atlas Accord, saw members of the US Special Forces travel to Mali to conduct training with local forces. "The participants were very attentive, and we were able to show them our tactics and see theirs as well," said Captain Bob Luther, a team leader with the 19th Special Forces Group.

The Collapse of Mali

As the US-backed war in Libya was taking down Qaddafi, nomadic Tuareg fighters in his service looted the regime's extensive weapons caches, crossed the border into their native Mali, and began to take over the northern part of that country. Anger within the country's armed forces over the democratically elected government's ineffective response to the rebellion resulted in a military coup. It was led by Amadou Sanogo, an officer who had received extensive training in the United States between 2004 and 2010 as part of the Pan-Sahel Initiative. Having overthrown the Malian democracy, he and his fellow officers proved even less effective in dealing with events in the north.

With the country in turmoil, the Tuareg fighters declared an independent state. Soon, however, heavily armed Islamist rebels from homegrown Ansar al-Dine as well as al-Qaeda in the Islamic Maghreb, Libya's Ansar al-Sharia, and Nigeria's Boko Haram, among others, pushed out the Tuaregs, took over much of the north, instituted a harsh brand of Shariah law, and created a humanitarian crisis that caused widespread suffering, sending refugees streaming from their homes.

These developments raised serious questions about the efficacy of US counterterrorism efforts. "This spectacular failure reveals that the US probably underestimated the complex sociocultural peculiarities of the region, and misread the realities of the terrain," Berny Sèbe, an expert on North and West Africa at the University of Birmingham in the United Kingdom, told me. "This led them to being grossly manipulated by local interests over which they had, in the end, very limited control."

Following a further series of Islamist victories and widespread atrocities, the French military intervened at the head of a coalition of Chadian, Nigerian, and other African troops, with support from the United States and the British. The foreign-led forces beat back the Islamists, who then shifted from conventional to guerrilla tactics, including suicide bombings.

In April, after such an attack killed three Chadian soldiers, that country's president announced that his forces, long supported by the United States through the Pan-Sahel Initiative, would withdraw from Mali. "Chad's army has no ability to face the kind of guerrilla fighting that is emerging," he said. In the meantime, the remnants of the US-backed Malian military fighting alongside the French were cited for gross human rights violations in their bid to retake control of their country.

After the French intervention in January, then–Secretary of Defense Leon Panetta said, "There is no consideration of putting any American boots on the ground at this time." Not long after, ten US military personnel were deployed to assist French and African forces, while twelve others were assigned to the embassy in the Malian capital, Bamako.

While he's quick to point out that Mali's downward spiral had much to do with its corrupt government, weak military, and rising levels of ethnic discontent, the Carnegie Endowment's Wehrey notes that the war in Libya was "a seismic event for the Sahel and the Sahara." Back from a fact-finding trip to Libya, he added that the effects of the revolution are already rippling far beyond the porous borders of Mali.

Wehrey cited recent findings by the United Nations Security Council's Group of Experts, which monitors an arms embargo imposed on Libya in 2011. "In the past 12 months," the panel reported, "the proliferation of weapons from Libya has continued at a worrying rate and has spread into new territory: West Africa, the Levant [the Eastern Mediterranean region], and potentially even the Horn of Africa. Illicit flows [of arms] from the country are fueling existing conflicts in Africa and the Levant and enriching the arsenals of a range of non-state actors, including terrorist groups."

Growing Instability

The collapse of Mali after a coup by an American-trained officer and Chad's flight from the fight in that country are just two indicators of how post-9/11 US military efforts in Africa have fared. "In two of the three other Sahelian states involved in the Pentagon's pan-Sahelian initiative, Mauritania and Niger, armies trained by the U.S., have also taken power in the past eight years," observed journalist William Wallis in the *Financial Times*. "In the third, Chad, they came close in a 2006 attempt." Still another coup plot involving members of the Chadian military was reportedly uncovered in the spring of 2013.

In March 2013, Major General Patrick Donahue, the commander of US Army Africa, told interviewer Gail McCabe that northwestern Africa was becoming increasingly "problematic." Al-Qaeda, he said, was at work destabilizing Algeria and Tunisia. The previous September, in fact, hundreds of Islamist protesters had attacked the US embassy compound in Tunisia, setting it on fire.

The US-backed French intervention in Mali also led to a revenge terror attack on the Amenas gas plant in Algeria. Carried out by the al-Mulathameen brigade, one of various new al-Qaeda in the Islamic Maghreb–linked militant groups emerging in the region, it led to the deaths of close to forty hostages, including three Americans. Planned by Mokhtar Belmokhtar, a veteran of the US-backed war against the Soviets in Afghanistan in the 1980s, it was only the first in a series of blowback responses to US and Western interventions in Northern Africa that may have far-reaching implications.

Belmokhtar's forces also teamed up with fighters from the Movement for Unity and Jihad in West Africa—yet another Islamist militant group of recent vintage—to carry out coordinated attacks on a French-run uranium mine and a nearby military base in Agadez, Niger, that killed at least twenty-five people. A mid-2013 attack on the French embassy in Libya by local militants was also seen as a reprisal for the French war in Mali.

According to Wehrey, the French military's push there had the additional effect of reversing the flow of militants, sending many back into Libya to recuperate and seek additional training. Nigerian Islamist fighters driven from Mali returned to their native land with fresh training and innovative tactics as well as heavy weapons from Libya. Increasingly battle-hardened, extremist Islamist insurgents from two Nigerian groups, Boko Haram and the newer, even more radical Ansaru, have escalated a long-simmering conflict in that West African oil giant.

For years, Nigerian forces have been trained and supported by the United States through the Africa Contingency Operations Training and Assistance program. The country has also been a beneficiary of US Foreign Military Financing, which provides grants and loans to purchase US-produced weaponry and equipment and funds military training. In recent years, however, brutal responses by Nigerian forces to what had been a fringe Islamist sect have transformed Boko Haram into a regional terrorist force.

The situation has grown so serious that President Goodluck Jonathan finally declared a state of emergency in northern Nigeria, after which Secretary of State John Kerry spoke out about "credible allegations that Nigerian security forces are committing gross human rights violations, which, in turn, only escalate the violence and fuel extremism." After a Boko Haram militant killed a soldier in the town of Baga, for example, Nigerian troops attacked the town, destroying more than 2,000 homes and killing an estimated 183 people.

Similarly, according to a recent United Nations report, the Congolese army's 391st Commando Battalion, formed with US support and trained for eight months by US Special Operations forces, later took part in mass rapes and other atrocities. Fleeing the advance of a brutal (non-Islamic) rebel group known as M23, its troops joined with other Congolese soldiers in raping close to one hundred women and more than thirty girls in November 2012.

"This magnificent battalion will set a new mark in this nation's continuing transformation of an army dedicated and committed to professionalism, accountability, sustainability, and meaningful security," said Brigadier General Christopher Haas, the head of US Special Operations Command Africa, in 2010 as the battalion graduated from training.

Earlier in 2013, incoming AFRICOM commander General David Rodriguez told the Senate Armed Services Committee that a review of the unit found its "officers and enlisted soldiers appear motivated, organized, and trained in small unit maneuver and tactics," even if there were "limited metrics to measure the battalion's combat effectiveness and performance in protecting civilians." The UN report told a different story. For example, it described "a 14 year old boy . . . shot dead on 25 November 2012 in the village of Kalungu, Kalehe territory, by a soldier of the 391 Battalion. The boy was returning from the fields when two soldiers tried to steal his goat. As he tried to resist and flee, one of the soldiers shot him."

Despite years of US military aid to the Democratic Republic of Congo, M23 has dealt its army heavy blows and, according to Rodriguez, is now destabilizing the region. But they haven't done it alone. According to Rodriguez, M23 "would not be the threat it is today without external support including evidence of support from the Rwandan government."

For years, the United States aided Rwanda through various programs, including the International Military Education and Training initiative and Foreign Military Financing. In 2012, the United States cut $200,000 in military assistance to Rwanda—a signal of its disapproval of that government's support for M23. Still, as Rodriguez admitted to the Senate earlier this year, the United States continues to "support Rwanda's participation in United Nations peacekeeping missions in Africa."

After years of US assistance, including support from Special Operations forces advisors, the Central African Republic's military was defeated and the country's president ousted by another newly formed rebel group known as Seleka. In short order, that country's army chiefs pledged their allegiance to the leader of the coup, while hostility on the part of the rebels forced the United States and its allies to suspend their hunt for Kony.

A strategic partner and bulwark of US counterterrorism efforts, Kenya receives around $1 billion in US aid annually and elements of its military have been trained by US Special Operations forces. But in September 2012, *Foreign Policy*'s Jonathan Horowitz reported on allegations of "Kenyan counterterrorism death squads . . . killing and disappearing people." Later, Human Rights Watch drew attention to the Kenyan military's response to a November attack by an unknown gunman that killed three soldiers in the northern town of Garissa. The "Kenyan army surrounded the town, preventing anyone from leaving or entering, and started attacking residents and traders," the group reported. "The witnesses said that the military shot at people, raped women, and assaulted anyone in sight."

Another longtime recipient of US support, the Ethiopian military, was also involved in abuses in 2012, following an attack by gunmen on a commercial farm. In response, according to Human

Rights Watch, members of Ethiopia's army raped, arbitrarily arrested, and assaulted local villagers.

The Ugandan military has been the primary US proxy when it comes to policing Somalia. Its members were, however, implicated in the beating and even killing of citizens during domestic unrest in 2011. Burundi has also received significant US military support, and high-ranking officers in its army have been linked to the illegal mineral trade, according to a report by the watchdog group Global Witness. Despite years of cooperation with the US military, Senegal appears more vulnerable to extremism and increasingly unstable, according to a report by the Institute of Security Studies.

And so it goes across the continent.

Success Stories

In addition to the Gulf of Guinea, AFRICOM's chief spokesman pointed to Somalia as another major US success story on the continent. It's true that Somalia is more stable now than it has been in years, even if a weakened al-Shabaab continues to carry out attacks. The spokesman even pointed to a recent CNN report about a trickle of tourists entering the war-torn country and the construction of a luxury beach resort in the capital, Mogadishu.

I asked for other AFRICOM success stories, but only those two came to his mind—and no one should be surprised by that.

After all, in 2006, before AFRICOM came into existence, eleven African nations were among the top twenty in the Fund for Peace's annual Failed States Index. By 2012, that number had risen to fifteen (sixteen if you count the new nation of South Sudan).

In 2001, according to the Global Terrorism Database from the National Consortium for the Study of Terrorism and Responses to Terrorism at the University of Maryland, there were 119 terrorist incidents in sub-Saharan Africa. By 2011, the last year for which numbers are available, there were close to 500. A recent report from the International Center for Terrorism Studies at the Potomac Institute for Policy Studies counted twenty-one terrorist attacks in the Maghreb and Sahel regions of Northern Africa in 2001. During the Obama years, the figures have fluctuated between 144 and 204 annually.

Similarly, an analysis of 65,000 individual incidents of political violence in Africa from 1997 to 2012, assembled by researchers affiliated with the International Peace Research Institute, found that "violent Islamist activity has increased significantly in the past 15 years, with a particular[ly] sharp increase witnessed from 2010 onwards." Additionally, according to researcher Caitriona Dowd, there is "evidence for the geographic spread of violent Islamist activity both south- and east-ward on the continent."

In fact, the trends appear stark and eerily mirror statements from AFRICOM's leaders.

In March 2009, after years of training indigenous forces and hundreds of millions of dollars spent on counterterrorism activities, General William Ward, the first leader of US Africa Command, gave its inaugural status report to the Senate Armed Services Committee. It was bleak. "Al-Qaeda," he said, "increased its influence dramatically across north and east Africa over the past three years with the growth of East Africa al-Qaeda, al-Shabaab, and al-Qaeda in the Lands of the Islamic Maghreb (AQIM)."

In February 2013, after four more years of military engagement, security assistance, training of indigenous armies, and hundreds of millions of dollars more in funding, AFRICOM's incoming commander General David Rodriguez explained the current situation to the Senate in even more ominous terms. "The command's number one priority is East Africa with particular focus on al-Shabaab and al-Qaeda networks. This is followed by violent extremist [movements] and al-Qaeda in North and West Africa and the Islamic Maghreb. AFRICOM's third priority is Counter-LRA [Lord's Resistance Army] operations."

Rodriguez warned that, "with the increasing threat of al-Qaeda in the Islamic Maghreb, I see a greater risk of regional instability if we do not engage aggressively." In addition to that group, he declared al-Shabaab and Boko Haram major menaces. He also mentioned the problems posed by the Movement for Unity and Jihad in West Africa and Ansar al-Dine. Libya, he told them, was threatened by "hundreds of disparate militias," while M23 was "destabilizing the entire Great Lakes region [of Central Africa]."

In West Africa, he admitted, there was also a major narcotics trafficking problem. Similarly, East Africa was "experiencing an increase in heroin trafficking across the Indian Ocean from Afghanistan and Pakistan." In addition, "in the Sahel region of North Africa, cocaine and hashish trafficking is being facilitated by, and directly benefitting, organizations like al-Qaeda in the Islamic Maghreb leading to increased regional instability."

In other words, ten years after Washington began pouring taxpayer dollars into counterterrorism and stability efforts across Africa and its forces first began operating from Camp Lemonnier, the continent has experienced profound changes, just not those the United States sought. The University of Birmingham's Berny Sèbe ticks off postrevolutionary Libya, the collapse of Mali, the rise of Boko Haram in Nigeria, the coup in the Central African Republic, and violence in Africa's Great Lakes region as evidence of increasing volatility. "The continent is certainly more unstable today than it was in the early 2000s, when the US. started to intervene more directly," he told me.

As the war in Afghanistan—a conflict born of blowback—winds down, there will be greater incentive and opportunity to project US military power in Africa. However, even a cursory reading of recent history suggests that this impulse is unlikely to achieve US goals. While correlation doesn't equal causation, there is ample evidence to suggest the United States has helped facilitate a terror diaspora, imperiling nations and endangering peoples across Africa. In the wake of 9/11, Pentagon officials were hard-pressed to show evidence of a major African terror threat. Today, the continent is thick with militant groups that are increasingly crossing borders, sowing insecurity, and throwing the limits of US power into broad relief. After ten years of US operations to promote stability by military means, the results have been the opposite. Africa has become blowback central.

3

AFRICOM's Gigantic "Small Footprint": The Pivot to Africa

September 5, 2013

They're involved in Algeria and Angola, Benin and Botswana, Burkina Faso and Burundi, Cameroon and the Cape Verde Islands. And that's just the ABCs of the situation. Skip to the end of the alphabet and the story remains the same: Senegal and the Seychelles, Togo and Tunisia, Uganda and Zambia. From north to south, east to west, the Horn of Africa to the Sahel, the heart of the continent to the islands off its coasts, the US military is at work. Base construction, security cooperation engagements, training exercises, advisory deployments, special operations missions, and a growing logistics network, all undeniable evidence of expansion—except at US Africa Command.

To hear AFRICOM tell it, US military involvement on the continent ranges from the minuscule to the microscopic. The command is adamant that Camp Lemonnier in Djibouti remains its single "military base" in all of Africa. The head of the command insists that the US military maintains a "small footprint" on the continent. AFRICOM's chief spokesman has consistently minimized the scope of its operations and the number of facilities it maintains or shares with host nations, asserting that only "a small presence of personnel who conduct short-duration engagements" are operating from "several locations" on the continent at any given time.

In recent years, Washington has very publicly proclaimed a "pivot to Asia," a "rebalancing" of its military resources eastward, without actually carrying out wholesale policy changes. Elsewhere, however, from the Middle East to South America, the Pentagon is increasingly engaged in shadowy operations whose details emerge piecemeal and are rarely examined in a comprehensive way. Nowhere is this truer than in Africa.

The proof is in the details—a seemingly ceaseless string of projects, operations, and engagements. Each mission, as AFRICOM insists, may be relatively limited and each footprint might be "small" on its own, but taken as a whole, US military operations are sweeping and expansive. Evidence of an American pivot to Africa is almost everywhere on the continent. Few, however, have paid much notice.

If the proverbial picture is worth a thousand words, then what's a map worth? Take, for instance, the one created by TomDispatch that documents US military outposts, construction, security cooperation, and deployments in Africa. It looks like a field of mushrooms after a monsoon. US Africa Command recognizes fifty-four countries on the continent, but refuses to say in which ones (or even in how many) it now conducts operations. An investigation by TomDispatch has found recent US military involvement with no fewer than forty-nine African nations.

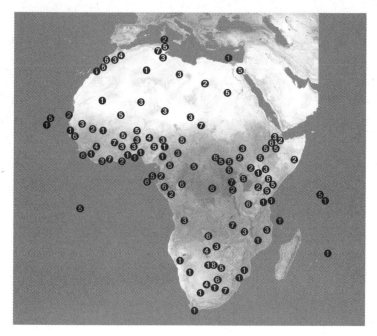

The US Military's Pivot to Africa, 2012–2013. ©2013 TomDispatch

Key

❶ US military training, advising, or tactical deployments during 2013
❷ US military training, advising, or tactical deployments during 2012
❸ US "security cooperation"
❹ Army National Guard partnerships
❺ US bases, forward operating sites (FOSes), contingency security locations
    (CSLs), contingency locations (CLs), airports with fueling agreements, and
    various shared facilities
❻ US military training/advising of indigenous troops carried out in a third
    country during 2013
❼ US military training/advising of indigenous troops carried out in a third
    country during 2012

In some, the United States maintains bases, even if under other names. In others, it trains local partners and proxies to battle militants. Elsewhere, it is building facilities for its allies or infrastructure for locals. Many African nations are home to multiple US military projects. Despite what AFRICOM officials say, a careful reading of internal briefings, contracts, and other official documents, as well as open-source information, including the command's own press releases and news items, reveals that military operations in Africa are already vast and will be expanding for the foreseeable future.

A Base by Any Other Name . . .

What does the US military footprint in Africa look like? Colonel Tom Davis, AFRICOM's Director of Public Affairs, is unequivocal: "Other than our base at Camp Lemonnier in Djibouti, we do not have military bases in Africa, nor do we have plans to establish any." He admits only that the United States has "temporary facilities elsewhere . . . that support much smaller numbers of personnel, usually for a specific activity."

AFRICOM's chief of media engagement Benjamin Benson echoes this, telling me that it's almost impossible to offer a list of forward operating bases. "Places that [US forces] might be, the range of possible locations can get really big, but can provide a really skewed image of where we are . . . versus other places where we have ongoing operations. So, in terms of providing a number, I'd be at a loss of how to quantify this."

A briefing prepared last year by Captain Rick Cook, the chief of AFRICOM's Engineering Division, tells a different story, making reference to forward operating sites or FOSs (long-term locations), cooperative security locations or CSLs (which troops

Entebbe Cooperative Security Location, Entebbe, Uganda, in 2009 (left) and 2013 (below). ©2013 Google ©2013 Digital Globe

periodically rotate in and out of), and contingency locations or CLs (which are used only during ongoing operations). A separate briefing prepared last year by Lieutenant Colonel David Knellinger references seven CSLs across Africa whose whereabouts are classified. A third briefing, produced in July 2012 by US Army Africa, identifies one of the CSL sites as Entebbe, Uganda, a location from which US contractors have flown secret surveillance missions using innocuous-looking, white Pilatus PC-12 turboprop airplanes, according to an investigation by the *Washington Post*.

US Army Africa briefing materials obtained from 2012 obtained by TomDispatch reference plans to build six new gates to the Entebbe compound, eleven new "containerized housing units," new guard stations, new perimeter and security fencing, enhanced security lighting, and new concrete access ramps, among other improvements. Satellite photos indicate that many, if not all, of these upgrades have indeed taken place.

A 2009 image (above top) shows a bare-bones compound of dirt and grass tucked away on a Ugandan air base with just a few aircraft surrounding it. A satellite photo of the compound from earlier this year (above bottom) shows a strikingly more built-up camp surrounded by a swarm of helicopters and white airplanes.

Initially, AFRICOM's Benjamin Benson refused to comment on the construction or the number of aircraft, insisting that the command had no "public information" about it. Confronted with the 2013 satellite photo, Benson reviewed it and offered a reply that neither confirmed nor denied that the site was a US facility, but cautioned me about using "uncorroborated data." (Benson failed to respond to my request to corroborate the data through a site visit.) "I have no way of knowing where the photo was taken and how it was modified," he told me. "Assuming the location is Entebbe, as you suggest, I would again argue that the aircraft could belong to anyone . . . It would be irresponsible of me to speculate on the missions, roles, or ownership of these aircraft." He went on to suggest, however, that the aircraft might belong to the United Nations Organization Stabilization Mission in the Democratic Republic of the Congo (MONUSCO) which does have a presence at the Entebbe air base.

This buildup may only be the beginning for Entebbe CSL. Recent contracting documents examined by TomDispatch indicate that AFRICOM is considering an additional surge of air assets there—specifically hiring a private contractor to provide further "dedicated fixed-wing airlift services for movement of Department of Defense (DoD) personnel and cargo in the Central African

Region." This mercenary air force would keep as many as three planes in the air at the same time on any given day, logging a total of about seventy to one hundred hours per week. If the military goes ahead with these plans, the aircraft would ferry troops, weapons, and other matériel within Uganda and to the Central African Republic, the Democratic Republic of Congo, and South Sudan.

Another key, if little noticed, US outpost in Africa is located in Ouagadougou, the capital of Burkina Faso. An airbase there serves as the home of a Joint Special Operations Air Detachment, as well as the Trans-Sahara Short Take-Off and Landing Airlift Support initiative. According to military documents, that initiative supports "high-risk activities" carried out by elite forces from Joint Special Operations Task Force Trans Sahara.

In July, Berry Aviation, a Texas-based longtime Pentagon contractor, was awarded a nearly $50 million contract to provide aircraft and personnel for "Trans-Sahara Short Take-Off and Landing services." Under the terms of the deal, Berry will "perform casualty evacuation, personnel airlift, cargo airlift, as well as personnel and cargo aerial delivery services throughout the Trans-Sahara of Africa," according to a statement from the company. Contracting documents indicate that Algeria, Burkina Faso, Cameroon, Chad, Libya, Mali, Mauritania, Morocco, Niger, Nigeria, Senegal, and Tunisia are the "most likely locations for missions."

Special Ops in Africa

Ouagadougou is just one site for expanding US air operations in Africa. In 2012, the 435th Military Construction Flight (MCF)—a rapid-response mobile construction team—revitalized an airfield in South Sudan for Special Operations Command Africa, according to the unit's commander, Lieutenant Alexander Graboski.

Before that, the team also "installed a runway lighting system to enable 24-hour operations" at the outpost. Graboski states that the air force's 435th MCF "has been called upon many times by Special Operations Command Africa to send small teams to perform work in austere locations." This trend looks as if it will continue. According to a briefing prepared in 2013 by Hugh Denny of the US Army Corps of Engineers, plans have been drawn up for Special Operations Command Africa "operations support" facilities to be situated in "multiple locations."

AFRICOM spokesman Benson refused to answer questions about SOCAFRICA facilities, and would not comment on the locations of missions by an elite, quick-response force known as Naval Special Warfare Unit 10 (NSWU 10). But according to Captain Robert Smith, the commander of Naval Special Warfare Group Two, NSWU 10 has been engaged "with strategic countries such as Uganda, Somalia, [and] Nigeria."

Captain J. Dane Thorleifson, NSWU 10's outgoing commander, recently mentioned deployments in six "austere locations" in Africa and "every other month contingency operations—Libya, Tunisia, [and] POTUS," evidently a reference to President Barack Obama's three-nation trip to Africa in July 2013. Thorleifson also said NSWU 10 had been involved in training "proxy" forces, specifically "building critical host nation security capacity; enabling, advising, and assisting our African CT [counterterror] partner forces so they can swiftly counter and destroy al-Shabab, AQIM [al-Qaeda in the Islamic Maghreb], and Boko Haram."

Nzara in South Sudan is one of a string of shadowy forward operating posts on the continent where US Special Operations forces have been stationed in recent years. Other sites include Obo and Djema in the Central Africa Republic and Dungu in the Democratic Republic of Congo. According to Lieutenant Colonel

Guillaume Beaurpere, the commander of the 3rd Battalion, 10th Special Forces Group, "advisory assistance at forward outposts was directly responsible for the establishment of combined operations fusion centers where military commanders, local security officials, and a host of international and non-governmental organizations could share information about regional insurgent activity and coordinate military activities with civil authorities."

Drone bases are also expanding. As the *New York Times* has noted, what began as the deployment of one Predator drone to Niger had expanded to encompass daily flights by one of two larger, more advanced Reaper remotely piloted aircraft, supported by 120 air force personnel.

When it comes to expanding US outposts in Africa, the navy has also been active. It maintains a forward operating location—manned mostly by Seabees, Civil Affairs personnel, and force-protection troops—known as Camp Gilbert in Dire Dawa, Ethiopia. Since 2004, US troops have been stationed at a Kenyan naval base known as Camp Simba at Manda Bay. AFRICOM's Benson portrayed operations there as relatively minor, typified by "short-term training and engagement activities." The sixty or so "core" troops stationed there, he said, are also primarily Civil Affairs, Seabees, and security personnel who take part in "military-to-military engagements with Kenyan forces and humanitarian initiatives."

An AFRICOM briefing in 2013 suggested, however, that the base is destined to be more than a backwater post. It called attention to improvements in water and power infrastructure and an extension of the runway at the airfield, as well as greater "surge capacity" for bringing in forces in the future. A second briefing, prepared by the navy and obtained by TomDispatch, details nine key infrastructure upgrades that are on the drawing board, under way, or completed.

In addition to extending and improving that runway, they include providing more potable water storage, latrines, and lodgings to accommodate a future "surge" of troops, doubling the capacity of washer and dryer units, upgrading dining facilities, improving roadways and boat ramps, providing fuel storage, and installing a new generator to handle additional demands for power. In a March 2013 article in the *National Journal*, James Kitfield, who visited the base, shed additional light on expansion there. "Navy Seabee engineers," he wrote, "have been working round-the-clock shifts for months to finish a runway extension before the rainy season arrives. Once completed, it will allow larger aircraft like C-130s to land and supply Americans or African Union troops."

AFRICOM's Benson tells TomDispatch that the US military also makes use of six buildings located on Kenyan military bases at the airport and seaport of Mombasa. In addition, he verified that it has used Léopold Sédar Senghor International Airport in Senegal for refueling stops as well as the "transportation of teams participating in security cooperation activities," such as training missions. He confirmed a similar deal for the use of Addis Ababa Bole International Airport in Ethiopia.

While Benson refused additional comment, official documents indicate that the United States has similar agreements for the use of Nsimalen Airport and Douala International Airport in Cameroon, Amílcar Cabral International Airport and Praia International Airport in Cape Verde, N'Djamena International Airport in Chad, Cairo International Airport in Egypt, Jomo Kenyatta International Airport and Moi International Airport in Kenya, Kotoka International Airport in Ghana, Marrakech-Menara Airport in Morocco, Nnamdi Azikiwe International Airport in Nigeria, Seychelles International Airport in the Seychelles, Sir Seretse Khama International Airport in Botswana, Bamako-Senou

International Airport in Mali, and Tunis-Carthage International Airport in Tunisia. All told, according to Sam Cooks, a liaison officer with the Defense Logistics Agency, the US military now has twenty-nine agreements to use international airports in Africa as refueling centers.

In addition, there is that sophisticated logistics system, officially known as the AFRICOM Surface Distribution Network but colloquially referred to as the "New Spice Route," that US Africa Command has built. It connects posts in Manda Bay, Garissa, and Mombasa in Kenya, Kampala and Entebbe in Uganda, Dire Dawa in Ethiopia, as well as crucial port facilities used by the navy's CTF-53 (Commander, Task Force, Five Three) in Djibouti, which are collectively referred to as "the port of Djibouti" by the military. Other key ports for the US military on the continent, according to Lieutenant Colonel Wade Lawrence of US Transportation Command, include Ghana's Tema and Senegal's Dakar.

The United States also maintains ten marine gas and oil bunker locations in eight African nations, according to the Defense Logistics Agency. AFRICOM's Benson refuses to name the countries, but recent military contracting documents list key fuel bunker locations in Douala, Cameroon; Mindelo, Cape Verde; Abidjan, Côte d'Ivoire; Port Gentil, Gabon; Sekondi, Ghana; Mombasa, Kenya; Port Luis, Mauritius; Walvis Bay, Namibia; Lagos, Nigeria; Port Victoria, Seychelles; Durban, South Africa; and Dar es Salaam, Tanzania.

The United States also continues to maintain a longtime Naval Medical Research Unit, known as NAMRU-3, in Cairo, Egypt. Another little-noticed medical investigation component, the US Army Research Unit—Kenya, operates from facilities in Kisumu and Kericho.

(In and) Out of Africa

When considering the scope and rapid expansion of US military activities in Africa, it's important to keep in mind that certain key "African" bases are actually located off the continent, which helps AFRICOM keep a semblance of a "light footprint" there. Its headquarters, as a start, isn't located on the continent at all, but at Kelley Barracks in Stuttgart-Moehringen, Germany. In June, *Süddeutsche Zeitung* reported that the Stuttgart base and the US Air Force's Air Operations Center in Ramstein, Germany, were both integral to drone operations in Africa.

Key logistics support hubs for AFRICOM are located in Rota, Spain; Aruba in the Lesser Antilles; and Souda Bay, Greece, as well as at Ramstein. The command also maintains a forward operating site on Britain's Ascension Island, located about 1,000 miles off the coast of Africa in the South Atlantic, but refused requests for further information about its role in operations.

Another important logistics facility is located in Sigonella on the island of Sicily. Italy, it turns out, is an especially crucial component of US operations in Africa. Special-Purpose Marine Air-Ground Task Force Africa, which provides teams of marines and sailors for "small-footprint theater security cooperation engagements" across the continent, is based at Naval Air Station Sigonella. According to Benson, it deployed personnel to Botswana, Liberia, Djibouti, Burundi, Uganda, Tanzania, Kenya, Tunisia, and Senegal.

In the future, U.S. Army Africa will be based at Caserma Del Din in northern Italy, adjacent to the recently completed home of the 173rd Airborne Brigade Combat Team. A 2012 US Army Africa briefing indicates that construction projects at the Caserma Del Din base will continue through 2018. The reported price-tag for the entire complex: $310 million.

A Big Base Gets Bigger

While that sum is sizable, it's surpassed by spending on the lone official US base on the African continent, Camp Lemonnier. That former French Foreign Legion post has been on a decade-long growth spurt.

In 2002, the United States dispatched personnel to Africa as part of Combined Joint Task Force–Horn of Africa. The next year, CJTF-HOA took up residence at Camp Lemonnier, where it resides to this day. In 2005, the United States struck a five-year land-use agreement with the Djibouti government and, in late 2010, exercised the first of two five-year renewal options. In 2006, the United States signed a separate agreement to expand the camp's boundaries to 500 acres.

According to Benson, between 2009 and 2012, $390 million was spent on construction there. In recent years, the outpost has been transformed by the addition of an electric power plant, enhanced water storage and treatment facilities, a dining hall, more facilities for Special Operations Command, and the expansion of aircraft taxiways and parking aprons.

A briefing prepared in 2013 by the Naval Facilities Engineering Command listed a plethora of projects currently under way or poised to begin, including an aircraft maintenance hangar, a telecommunications facility, a fire station, additional security fencing, an ammunition supply facility, interior paved roads, a general-purpose warehouse, maintenance shelters for aircraft, an aircraft logistics apron, taxiway enhancements, expeditionary lodging, a combat aircraft loading apron, and a taxiway extension on the east side of the airfield.

Navy documents detailed the price tag for 2013's proposed projects, including $7.5 million to be spent on containerized living

Plans for construction of the Special Operations or "Task Force" Compound at Camp Lemonnier, Djibouti

units and workspaces, $22 million for cold storage and the expansion of dining facilities, $27 million for a fitness center, $43 million for a joint headquarters facility, and a whopping $220 million for a Special Operations Compound, also referred to as "Task Force Compound."

According to a 2012 briefing by Knellinger, the Special Operations Compound will eventually hold at least eighteen new facilities, including a two-story joint operations center, a two-story tactical operations center, two five-story barracks, a large motor pool facility, a supply warehouse, and an aircraft hangar with an adjacent air operations center.

A document produced by Lieutenant Troy Gilbert, an infrastructure planner with AFRICOM's engineer division, listed almost $400 million in "emergency" military construction at Camp Lemonnier, including work on the special operations compound and more than $150 million for a new combat aircraft loading area. Navy documents, for their part, estimate that construction at Camp Lemonnier will continue at $70 million to $100 million annually, with future projects to include a $20 million wastewater treatment plant, a $40 million medical and dental center, and more than $150 million in troop housing.

Rules of Engagement

In addition, the US military has been supporting construction all over Africa for its allies. A report by Hugh Denny of the Army Corps of Engineers referenced seventy-nine such projects in thirty-three countries between 2011 and 2013, including Benin, Botswana, Burkina Faso, Cameroon, Cape Verde, Chad, Côte d'Ivoire, Djibouti, Ethiopia, Ghana, Guinea, Kenya, Lesotho, Liberia, Malawi, Mali, Mauritania, Mauritius, Mozambique, Niger, Nigeria, Rwanda, Senegal, Sierra Leone, Swaziland, Tanzania, Tunisia, The Gambia, Togo, Uganda, and Zambia. The reported price tag: $48 million.

Senegal has, for example, received a $1.2 million "peacekeeping operations training center" under the auspices of the US Africa Contingency Operations Training and Assistance (ACOTA) program. ACOTA has also supported training center projects in Benin, Burkina Faso, Burundi, Djibouti, Ethiopia, Kenya, Malawi, Nigeria, Niger, Rwanda, Sierra Leone, South Africa, Tanzania, Togo, and Uganda.

The United States is planning to finance the construction of barracks and other facilities for Ghana's armed forces. AFRICOM's Benson also confirmed to TomDispatch that the US Army Corps of Engineers has plans to "equip and refurbish five military border security posts in Djibouti along the Somalia/Somaliland border." In Kenya, US Special Operations forces have "played a crucial role in infrastructure investments for the Kenyan Special Operations Regiment and especially in the establishment of the Kenyan Ranger school," according to Lieutenant Colonel Guillaume Beaurpere of the 3rd Battalion, 10th Special Forces Group.

AFRICOM's "humanitarian assistance" program is also expansive. A 2013 navy briefing listed $7.1 million in humanitarian construction projects—like schools, orphanages, and medical facilities—in nineteen countries from Comoros to Guinea-Bissau to Rwanda. Denny's report also listed nine Army Corps of Engineers "security assistance" efforts, valued at more than $12 million, carried out during 2012 and 2013, as well as fifteen additional "security cooperation" projects worth more than $22 million in countries across Africa.

A Deluge of Deployments

In addition to creating or maintaining bases and engaging in military construction across the continent, the United States is involved in near-constant training and advisory missions. According to AFRICOM's Colonel Tom Davis, the command was slated to carry out fourteen major bilateral and multilateral exercises by the end of 2013 alone. These were to include Saharan Express 2013, which brought together forces from Cape Verde, Côte d'Ivoire, Gambia, Liberia, Mauritania, Morocco, Senegal, and Sierra Leone, among other nations, for maritime security training; Obangame Express 2013, a counter-piracy exercise involving the armed forces of many nations, including Benin, Cameroon, Côte d'Ivoire, Equatorial Guinea, Gabon, Nigeria, Republic of Congo, São Tomé and Príncipe, and Togo; and Africa Endeavor 2013, in which the militaries of Djibouti, Burundi, Côte d'Ivoire, Zambia, and thirty-four other African nations took part.

And that's just the tip of the iceberg. As Davis told Tom-Dispatch, "We also conduct some type of military training or military-to-military engagement or activity with nearly every country on the African continent." A look at just some of the US missions in the spring of 2013 drives home the true extent of the growing US engagement in Africa.

In January, for instance, the US Air Force began transporting French troops to Mali to counter Islamist forces there. At a facility in Nairobi, Kenya, AFRICOM provided military intelligence training to junior officers from Kenya, Uganda, Burundi, Ethiopia, Tanzania, and South Sudan. In January and February, Special Operations forces personnel conducted a joint exercise code-named Silent Warrior with Cameroonian soldiers. February saw South African troops travel all the way to Chiang Mai, Thailand, to take part in Cobra Gold 2013, a multinational training exercise cosponsored by the US military.

In March, navy personnel worked with members of Cape Verde's armed forces, while Kentucky National Guard troops spent a week advising soldiers from the Comoros Islands. That same month, members of Special-Purpose Marine Air-Ground Task Force Africa deployed to the Singo Peace Support Training Center in Uganda to work with Ugandan soldiers prior to their assignment to the African Union Mission in Somalia. Over the course of the spring, members of the task force also mentored troops in Burundi, Cameroon, Ghana, Burkina Faso, the Seychelles, Mozambique, Tanzania, and Liberia.

In April, members of the task force also began training Senegalese commandos at Bel-Air military base in Dakar, while navy personnel deployed to Mozambique to school civilians in demining techniques. Meanwhile, marines traveled to Morocco to conduct a training exercise code-named African Lion 13 with that country's military. In May, army troops were sent to Lomé, Togo, to work with members of the Togolese Defense Force, as well as to Senga Bay, Malawi, to instruct soldiers there.

That month, navy personnel also conducted a joint exercise in the Mediterranean Sea with their Egyptian counterparts. In June, personnel from the Kentucky National Guard deployed to Djibouti to advise members of that country's military on border security methods, while Seabees teamed up with the Tanzanian People's Defense Force to build maritime security infrastructure. That same month, the air force airlifted Liberian troops to Bamako, Mali, to conduct a six-month peacekeeping operation.

Limited or Limitless?

Counting countries in which it has bases or outposts or has done construction, and those with which it has conducted military exercises, advisory assignments, security cooperation, or training missions, the US military, according to TomDispatch's analysis, is involved with more than 90 percent of Africa's fifty-four nations. While AFRICOM commander David Rodriguez maintains that the United States has only a "small footprint" on the continent, following those small footprints across the continent can be a breathtaking task.

It's not hard to imagine why the US military wants to maintain that "small footprint" fiction. On occasion, military commanders couldn't have been clearer on the subject. "A direct and overt presence of U.S. forces on the African continent can cause consternation . . . with our own partners who take great pride in their post-colonial abilities to independently secure themselves," wrote Beaurpere earlier this year in the military trade publication *Special Warfare*. Special Operations forces, he added, "must train to operate discreetly within these constraints and the cultural norms of the host nation."

On a visit to the Pentagon earlier this summer, AFRICOM's Rodriguez echoed the same point in candid comments to Voice of America: "The history of the African nations, the colonialism, all those things are what point to the reasons why we should . . . just use a small footprint."

Yet however useful that imagery may be to the Pentagon, the US military no longer has a small footprint in Africa. Even the repeated claims that US troops conduct only short-term, intermittent missions there has been officially contradicted. This July, at a change of command ceremony for NSWU 10, a spokesman noted the creation and implementation of "a five-year engagement strategy that encompassed the transition from episodic training events to regionally focused and persistent engagements in five Special Operations Command Africa priority countries."

In a question-and-answer piece in *Special Warfare*, Colonel John Deedrick, the commander of the 10th Special Forces Group, sounded off about his unit's area of responsibility: "We are widely employed throughout the continent. These are not episodic activities. We are there 365-days-a-year to share the burden, assist in shaping the environment, and exploit opportunities."

Exploitation and "persistent engagement" are exactly what critics of US military involvement in Africa have long feared, while blowback and the unforeseen consequences of US military action on the continent have already contributed to catastrophic destabilization.

Despite some candid admissions by officers involved in shadowy operations, AFRICOM continues to insist that troop deployments are highly circumscribed. The command will not, however, allow independent observers to make their own assessments.

Benson said CJTF-HOA does not "have a media visit program to regularly host journalists there."

My own requests to report on US operations on the continent were rejected in short order. "We will not make an exception in this case," Benson wrote in an email and followed up by emphasizing that US forces are deployed in Africa only "on a limited and temporary basis." TomDispatch's own analysis—and a mere glance at the map of recent missions—indicates that there are, in fact, very few limits on where the US military operates in Africa.

While Washington talks openly about rebalancing its military assets to Asia, a pivot to Africa is quietly and unmistakably under way. With the ever-present possibility of blowback from shadowy operations on the continent, the odds are that the results of that pivot will become increasingly evident, whether or not Americans recognize them as such. While behind closed doors, the military says: "Africa is the battlefield of tomorrow, today," it remains to be seen just when they'll say the same to the American people.

4

American Proxy Wars in Africa: A New Model for Expeditionary Warfare

March 13, 2014

Lion Forward Teams? Echo Casemate? Juniper Micron?

You could be forgiven if this jumble of words looks like nonsense to you. It isn't. It's the language of the US military's simmering African interventions; the patois that goes with a set of missions carried out in countries most Americans couldn't locate on a map, the argot of conflicts now primarily fought by proxies and a former colonial power on a continent that the US military views as a hotbed of instability and that hawkish pundits increasingly see as a growth area for future armed interventions.

Yet over the past years, the results have often confounded the planning—with American operations serving as a catalyst for blowback. A US-backed uprising in Libya, for instance, helped spawn hundreds of militias that have increasingly caused chaos in that country, leading to repeated attacks on Western interests. Tunisia has become ever more destabilized, according to a top US commander in the region. Kenya and Algeria were hit by spectacular, large-scale terrorist attacks that left Americans dead or wounded. South Sudan, a fledgling nation Washington helped foster into being, has slipped into civil war. It now has more than 870,000 displaced persons, is facing an imminent hunger crisis, and has recently been the site of mass atrocities, including rapes and killings. Meanwhile, the US-backed military of Mali was repeatedly defeated by insurgent forces after managing to overthrow the elected government, and the US-supported forces of the Central African Republic (CAR) failed to stop a ragtag rebel group from ousting their president.

In an effort to stanch the bleeding in those latter two countries, the United States has been developing a back-to-the-future military policy by making common cause with one of the continent's former European colonial powers in a set of wars that seem to be spreading, not stanching violence and instability.

The French Connection

After establishing a trading post in present-day Senegal in 1659, France gradually undertook a conquest of West Africa that by the early twentieth century left it with a vast colonial domain encompassing present-day Burkina Faso, Benin, Chad, Guinea, Côte d'Ivoire, Mali, Niger, and Senegal, among other places. In the process, the French used Foreign Legionnaires from Algeria, *Goumiers* from Morocco, and *Tirailleurs* from Senegal, among other African troops, to bolster its ranks. Today, the United States is pioneering a twenty-first-century brand of expeditionary warfare that involves backing both France and the armies of its former colonial charges as Washington tries to accomplish its policy aims in Africa with a limited expenditure of blood and treasure.

In an op-ed piece for the *Washington Post*, President Barack Obama and French president François Hollande outlined their efforts in glowing terms:

> In Mali, French and African Union forces —with U.S. logistical and information support— have pushed back al-Qaeda-linked insurgents, allowing the people of Mali to pursue a democratic future. Across the Sahel, we are partnering with countries to prevent al-Qaeda from gaining new footholds. In the Central African Republic, French and African Union soldiers—backed by American airlift and support—are working to stem violence and create space for dialogue, reconciliation, and swift progress to transitional elections.

Missing from their joint piece, however, was any hint of the Western failures that helped facilitate the debacles in Mali and the Central African Republic, the continued crises plaguing those nations, or the potential for mission creep, unintended consequences, and future blowback from this new brand of coalition warfare. The US military, for its part, isn't saying much about current efforts in these two African nations, but official documents obtained by TomDispatch through the Freedom of Information Act offer telling details, while experts are sounding alarms about the ways in which these military interventions have already fallen short or failed.

Operation Juniper Micron

After 9/11, through programs like the Pan-Sahel Initiative and the Trans-Saharan Counterterrorism Partnership, the United States has pumped hundreds of millions of dollars into training and arming the militaries of Mali, Niger, Chad, Mauritania, Nigeria, Senegal, Morocco, Algeria, and Tunisia to promote "stability." In 2013, Captain J. Dane Thorleifson described such efforts as training "proxy" forces to build "critical host nation security capacity; enabling, advising, and assisting our African CT [counterterror] partner forces so they can swiftly counter and destroy al-Shabab, AQIM [al-Qaeda in the Islamic Maghreb], and Boko Haram." In other words, the US military is in the business of training African armies as the primary tactical forces combating local Islamic militant groups.

The first returns on Washington's new and developing form of "light footprint" warfare in Africa have hardly been stellar. After US and French forces helped topple Libyan dictator Muammar Gaddafi in 2011, neighboring Mali went from bulwark to basket case. In January 2013, former colonial power France launched a military intervention, code-named Operation Serval, to push back and defeat the Islamists who had muscled aside Tuareg rebels and were in the process of defeating a junta led by a US-trained Malian military officer.

At its peak, 4,500 French troops were fighting alongside West African forces, known as the African-led International Support Mission in Mali (AFISMA), later subsumed into a UN-mandated Multidimensional Integrated Stabilization Mission in Mali (MINUSMA). The AFISMA force, as detailed in an official US Army Africa briefing on training missions obtained by TomDispatch, reads like a who's who of American proxy forces in West Africa: Niger, Guinea, Burkina Faso, Côte d'Ivoire, Togo, Senegal, Benin, Liberia, Chad, Nigeria, Gambia, Ghana, and Sierra Leone.

Under the moniker Juniper Micron, the US military supported France's effort, airlifting its soldiers and matériel into Mali, flying refueling missions in support of its air power, and providing

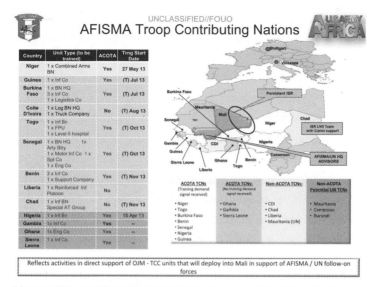

US Army Africa briefing slide detailing US efforts to aid the African-led International Support Mission in Mali (AFISMA).

"intelligence, surveillance, and reconnaissance" (ISR) through drone operations out of Base Aerienne 101 at Diori Hamani International Airport in Niamey, the capital of neighboring Niger. A US Army Africa AFISMA document on these operations also makes reference to the deployment to Chad of an ISR liaison team with communications support. Despite repeated pledges that it would put no boots on the ground in troubled Mali, in the spring of 2013, the Pentagon sent a small contingent to the US embassy in Bamako and other troops to support French and MINUSMA troops.

After issuing five media releases between January and March 2013 about efforts to aid the military mission in Mali, AFRICOM simply stopped talking about it. With rare exceptions, media coverage of the operation also dried up. In June, at a joint press conference with President Obama, Senegal's president Macky Sall did let slip that the United States was providing "almost all the food and fuel used by MINUSMA" as well as "intervening to assist us with the logistics after the French response."

A January 2014 *Stars and Stripes* article mentioned that the U.S. air refueling mission supporting the French, run from a US airbase in Spain, had already "distributed 15.6 million gallons of fuel, logging more than 3,400 flying hours" and that the effort would continue. In February, according to military reports, elements of the Air Force's 351st Expeditionary Refueling Squadron delivered their millionth pound of fuel to French fighter aircraft conducting operations over Mali. A December 2013 briefing document obtained by TomDispatch also mentions 181 US troops, the majority of them air force personnel, supporting Operation Juniper Micron.

Eager to learn where things stood today, I asked Benjamin Benson about the operation. "We're continuing to support and enable the French and international partners to confront AQIM and its affiliates in Mali," he told me. He then mentioned four key current mission sets being carried out by US forces: information sharing, intelligence and reconnaissance, planning and liaison teams, and aerial refueling and the airlifting of allied African troops.

US Army Africa documents obtained by TomDispatch offer further details about Operation Juniper Micron, including the use of Lion Forward Teams in support of that mission. I asked Benson for information about these small detachments that aided the French effort from Chad and from within Mali itself. "I don't have anything on that," was all he would say. A separate briefing slide, produced for an army official last year, noted that the US military provided support for the French mission from Rota and Morón, Spain; Ramstein, Germany; Sigonella, Italy; Kidal and Bamako, Mali; Niamey, Niger; Ouagadougou, Burkina Faso; and N'Djamena,

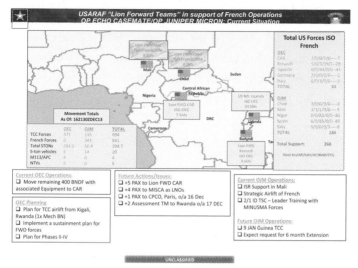

December 2013 US military document detailing American efforts to support French military operations in Mali and Central African Republic.

Chad. Benson refused to offer information about specific activities conducted from these locations, preferring to speak about air operations from unspecified locations and only in generalities.

Official military documents obtained by TomDispatch detail several US missions in support of proxy forces from the Multidimensional Integrated Stabilization Mission in Mali, including a scheduled eight weeks of predeployment training for troops from Niger in the summer of 2013, five weeks for Chadian forces in the autumn, and eight weeks in the autumn as well for Guinean soldiers, who would be sent into the Malian war zone. I asked Benson about plans for the training of African forces designated for MINUSMA in 2014. "In terms of the future on that . . . I don't know," was all he would say.

Another official briefing slide produced by US Army Africa notes, however, that from January through March 2014, the United States planned to send scores of trainers to prepare 1,400

Chadian troops for missions in Mali. Over the same months, other US personnel were to team up with French military trainers to ready an 850-man Guinean infantry force for similar service. Requests for further information from the French military about this and other missions were unanswered.

Operation Echo Casemate

Last spring, despite years of US assistance, including support from Special Operations forces advisors, the Central African Republic's military was swiftly defeated and the country's president ousted by Seleka, a mostly Muslim rebel group. Months of violence followed, with Seleka forces involved in widespread looting, rape, and murder. The result was growing sectarian clashes between the country's Muslim and Christian communities and the rise of Christian "anti-balaka" militias. (*Balaka* means machete in the local Sango language.) These militias have, in turn, engaged in an orgy of atrocities and ethnic cleansing directed against Muslims.

In December, backed by a United Nations Security Council resolution and in a bid to restore order, France sent troops into its former colony to bolster peacekeepers from the African-led International Support Mission in the Central African Republic (MISCA). As with the Mali mission, the United States joined the effort, pledging up to $60 million in military aid, pouring money into a trust fund for MISCA, and providing airlift services, as well as training African forces for deployment in the country.

Dubbed Echo Casemate, the operation—staged out of Burundi and Uganda—saw the US military airlift hundreds of Burundian troops, tons of equipment, and more than a dozen military vehicles into that strife-torn land in just the first five days of the mission, according to an AFRICOM media release. In

TCC Training

Chad	Guinea
Who: USARAF w/ up to 70* personnel from 2/1 HBCT	**Who:** USARAF w/ 35 personnel from 2/1 HBCT in coordination with French Army trainers in Senegal.
What: Conduct pre-deployment training model for a 1,400-man Chadian Infantry (1x UN IN BN, 1x UN Reserve BN)	**What:** Conduct a 60 day pre-deployment training model for a 850-man Guinean Infantry Contingent (2x motorized IN companies to deploy under Senegalese C2, 1x 425-man Reserve BN),
Where: Loumia, Chad	
When: Jan-Mar 14	**Where:** Kindia, Guinea
Why: Chad requested U.S. Army assistance to train its pre-deployment training of UN-led Multidimensional Stabilization Mission in Mali and demonstrate its capability to generate forces to promote regional stability.	**When:** 9-22 Dec 13 / 11 Jan – 3 Mar 14
	Why: Guinea requested U.S. Army assistance to prepare the Guinean units. First large scale training effort since Guinea has come off sanctions and committed to becoming a TCC for UN PKO missions.
* Contingent upon French contractor SGF participation	

As of: 19 Dec 13   UNCLASSIFIED   13

Official briefing slide with details on US training for Chad and Guinea—"troop contributing countries" aiding the US-supported military mission in Mali.

January, at France's request, the United States began airlifting a Rwandan mechanized battalion and 1,000 tons of their gear in from that country's capital, Kigali, via a staging area in Entebbe, Uganda (where the United States maintains a "cooperative security location" and from which US contractors had previously flown secret surveillance missions).

Asked about US training efforts, Benson was guarded. "I don't have that off the top of my head," he told me. "We do training with a lot of different countries in Africa." He offered little detail about the size and scope of the US effort, but a December 2013 briefing document obtained by TomDispatch mentions eighty-four US personnel, the majority of them based in Burundi, supporting Operation Echo Casemate. The *New York Times* reported that the United States "refrained from putting American boots on the ground" in the Central African Republic, but the document clearly indicates that a Lion Forward Team of army personnel was indeed sent there.

Another US Army Africa document produced late in 2013 noted that the United States provided military support for the French mission in that country from facilities in Germany, Italy, Uganda, Burundi, and the Central African Republic itself. It mentions plans to detail liaison officers to the MISCA mission and the Centre de planification et de conduite des opérations (the Joint Operations, Planning, and Command and Control Center) in Paris.

As US personnel deploy to Europe as part of Washington's African wars, additional European troops headed for Africa. In February 2014, for instance, another of the continent's former colonial powers, Germany, announced that some of its troops would be sent to Mali as part of a Franco-German brigade under the aegis of the European Union (EU) and would also aid in supporting an EU "peacekeeping mission" in the Central African Republic. Already, a host of other former imperial powers on the continent—including Belgium, Italy, the Netherlands, Portugal, Spain, and the United Kingdom—were part of a European Union training mission to school the Malian military. In January 2014, France announced that it was reorganizing its roughly 3,000 troops in Africa's Sahel region to reinforce a logistical base in Abidjan, the capital of Côte d'Ivoire; transform N'Djamena, Chad, into a hub for French fighter jets; concentrate special operations forces in Burkina Faso; and run drone missions out of Niamey, Niger (already a US hub for such missions).

Scrambling Africa

Operations by French and African forces, bolstered by the US military, beat back the Islamic militants in Mali and allowed presidential elections to be held. At the same time, the intervention caused a veritable terror diaspora that helped lead to attacks in Algeria, Niger, and Libya, without resolving Mali's underlying instability.

Writing in the most recent issue of the *CTC Sentinel*, analyst Bruce Whitehouse points out that the Malian government has yet to reassert its authority in the north of the country, reform its armed forces, tackle graft, or strengthen the rule of law: "Until major progress is made in each of these areas, little can be done to reduce the threat of terrorism . . . the underlying causes of Mali's 2012 instability—disaffection in the north, a fractured military, and systemic corruption—have yet to be fully addressed by the Malian government and its international partners."

The situation may be even worse in the Central African Republic. "When France sent troops to halt violence between Christians and Muslims in Central African Republic," John Irish and Daniel Flynn of Reuters reported in early 2014, "commanders named the mission Sangaris after a local butterfly to reflect its short life. Three months later, it is clear they badly miscalculated." Instead, violence had escalated, more than one million people had been displaced, tens of thousands had been killed, looting had occurred on a massive scale, and in February 2014 US Director of National Intelligence James Clapper informed Congress that "much of the country has devolved into lawlessness."

It is also quickly becoming a regional arms-smuggling hot spot. With millions of weapons reportedly unaccounted for as a result of the pillaging of government armories, it's feared that weaponry will find its way into other continental crisis zones, including Nigeria, Libya, and the Democratic Republic of Congo.

In addition, the coalition operation there has failed to prevent what, after a visit to the largely lawless capital city of Bangui, the United Nations High Commissioner for Refugees Antonio

Guterres called "ethnic-religious cleansing." Amnesty International found much the same. "Once vibrant Muslim communities in towns and cities throughout the country have been completely destroyed as all Muslim members have either been killed or driven away. Those few left behind live in fear that they will be attacked by anti-balaka groups in their towns or on the roads," the human rights group reported. "While an African Union peacekeeping force, the African-led International Support Mission to the Central African Republic (MISCA), supported by French troops, has been deployed in the country since early December 2013, they have failed to adequately protect civilians and prevent the current ethnic cleansing from taking place."

French Wine in New Bottles?

"We're not involved with the fighting in Mali," AFRICOM spokesman Benson told me, emphasizing that the US military was not engaged in combat there. But Washington is increasingly involved in the growing wars for West and Central Africa. Just about every move it has made in the region thus far has helped spread conflict and chaos, while contributing to African destabilization. Worse yet, no end to this process appears to be in sight. Despite building up the manpower of its African proxies and being backed by the US military's logistical might, France has not completed its mission in Mali and will be keeping troops there to conduct counterrorism operations for the foreseeable future.

Similarly, the French were also forced to send reinforcements into the Central African Republic (and the UN has called for still more troops), while Chadian MISCA forces have been repeatedly accused of attacking civilians. In a sign that the US-backed French military mission to Africa could spread, the Nigerian government is now requesting French troops to help it halt increasingly deadly attacks by Boko Haram militants who have gained strength and weaponry in the wake of the unrest in Libya, Mali, and the Central African Republic (and have reportedly also spread into Niger, Chad, and Cameroon). On top of this, Clapper recently reported that Chad, Niger, Mali, and Mauritania were endangered by their support of the French-led effort in Mali and at risk of increased terror attacks "as retribution."

Still, this seems to have changed little for the director of national intelligence. "Leveraging and partnering with the French is a way to go," he told Congress. "They have insight and understanding and, importantly, a willingness to use the forces they have there now."

France has indeed exhibited a long-standing willingness to use military force in Africa, but what "insight and understanding" its officials gleaned from this experience is an open question. One hundred sixteen years after it completed its conquest of what was then French Sudan, France's forces are again fighting and dying on the same fields of battle, though today the country is called Mali. Again and again during the early twentieth century, France launched military expeditions, including during the 1928–1931 Kongo-Wara rebellion, against indigenous peoples in French Equatorial Africa. Today, France's soldiers are being killed on the same ground in what's now known as the Central African Republic. It looks as if they may be slogging on in these nations, in partnership with the US military, for years to come, with no evident ability to achieve lasting results.

A new type of expeditionary warfare is under way in Africa, but there's little to suggest that America's backing of a former colonial power will ultimately yield the long-term successes that years of support for local proxies could not. So far, the United

States has been willing to let European and African forces do the fighting, but if these interventions drag on and the violence continues to leap from country to country as yet more militant groups morph and multiply, the risk only rises of Washington wading ever deeper into postcolonial wars with an eerily colonial look. "Leveraging and partnering with the French" may be the current way to go, according to Washington. Just where it's going is the real question.

5

Nonstop Ops in Africa: US Military Averaging More Than a Mission a Day in Africa

March 27, 2014

The numbers tell the story: 10 exercises, 55 operations, 481 security cooperation activities.

For years, the US military has publicly insisted that its efforts in Africa are small scale. They have, however, balked at specifying just what their claimed "light footprint" on the continent actually consists of. During an interview, for instance, a US Africa Command (AFRICOM) spokesman once expressed worry to me that tabulating the command's deployments would offer a "skewed image" of US efforts there.

It turns out that the numbers do just the opposite.

In 2013, according to AFRICOM commander General David Rodriguez, the US military carried out a total of 546 "activities" on the continent—a catchall term for everything the military does in

Africa. In other words, it averages about one and a half missions a day. This represents a 217 percent increase in operations, programs, and exercises since the command was established in 2008.

In testimony before the Senate Armed Services Committee, Rodriguez noted that the 10 exercises, 55 operations, and 481 security cooperation activities made AFRICOM "an extremely active geographic command." But exactly what the command is "active" in doing is often far from clear.

AFRICOM releases information about only a fraction of its activities. It offers no breakdown on the nature of its operations. And it allows only a handful of cherry-picked reporters the chance to observe a few select missions. The command refuses even to release a count of the countries in which it is "active," preferring to keep most information about what it's doing—and when and where—secret.

While Rodriguez's testimony offers only a glimpse of the scale of its activities, a cache of previously undisclosed military briefing documents obtained by TomDispatch sheds additional light on the types of missions being carried out and their locations across the continent. These briefings prepared for top commanders and civilian officials in 2013 demonstrate a substantial increase in deployments in recent years and reveal military operations to be more extensive than previously reported. They also indicate that the pace of operations in Africa will remain robust in 2014, with US forces expected again to average far more than a mission each day on the continent.

The Constant Gardener

The US military carries out a wide range of operations in Africa, but above all, it conducts training missions, mentoring allies and funding, equipping, and advising its local surrogates.

US Africa Command describes its activities as advancing "U.S. national security interests through focused, sustained engagement with partners" and insists that its "operations, exercises, and security cooperation assistance programs support U.S. Government foreign policy and do so primarily through military-to-military activities and assistance programs."

Saharan Express is a typical exercise that biennially pairs US forces with members of the navies and coast guards of around a dozen mostly African countries. Other operations include Juniper Micron and Echo Casemate, missions focused on aiding French and African interventions in Mali and the Central African Republic. Other "security cooperation" activities include the State Partnership Program, which teams African military forces with US National Guard units and the State Department–funded Africa Contingency Operations Training and Assistance (ACOTA) program through which American mentors and advisors provide equipment and instruction to African units.

Many military-to-military activities and advisory missions are carried out by soldiers from the Army's 2nd Brigade Combat Team, 1st Infantry Division, as part of a "regionally aligned forces" effort that farms out specially trained US troops to geographic combatant commands like AFRICOM. Other training engagements are carried out by units from across the service branches, including Africa Partnership Station 13, whose US naval personnel and marines teach skills such as patrolling procedures and hand-to-hand combat techniques. Meanwhile, members of the air force recently provided assistance to Nigerian troops in areas ranging from logistics to airlift support to public affairs.

Previously undisclosed U.S. Army Africa records reveal a 94 percent increase in all activities by army personnel from 2011 to 2013, including a 174 percent surge in State Partnership missions

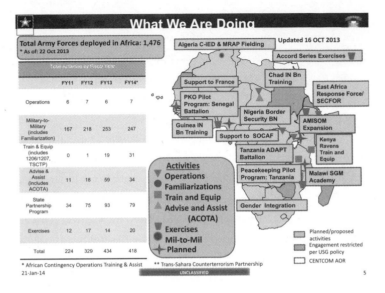

(from thirty-four to ninety-three) and a 436 percent jump in Advise-and-Assist activities including ACOTA missions (from eleven to fifty-nine). According to an Army Africa document from December 2013, efforts that year involved everything from teaching Kenyan troops how to use Raven surveillance drones and helping Algerian forces field new mine-resistant ambush-protected vehicles, or MRAPS, to training Chadian and Guinean infantrymen and aiding France's ongoing interventions in West and Central Africa.

AFRICOM's Benjamin Benson refused to offer further details about these activities. "We do training with a lot of different countries in Africa," he told me. When I asked if he had a number on those "different countries," he replied, "No, I don't." But a cache of records detailing deployments by members of just the 2nd Brigade Combat Team, 1st Infantry Division, from June through December 2013, highlights the sheer size, scope, and sweep of such training missions.

June saw members of the 2nd Brigade Combat Team deployed to Niger, Uganda, Ghana, and on two separate missions to Malawi; in July, troops from the team traveled to Burundi, Mauritania, Niger, Uganda, and South Africa; August deployments included the Democratic Republic of Congo, Kenya, South Africa, Niger, two missions in Malawi, and three to Uganda; September saw activities in Chad, Togo, Cameroon, Ghana, São Tomé and Príncipe, Sierra Leone, Guinea, Uganda, and Malawi; in October, members of the unit headed for Guinea and South Africa; November's deployments consisted of Lesotho, Ethiopia, Tanzania, Uganda, and Guinea; while December's schedule involved activities in South Sudan, Cameroon, and Uganda. All told, the 2nd Brigade Combat Team, 1st Infantry Division carried out 128 separate "activities" in twenty-eight African countries during all of 2013.

The records obtained by TomDispatch also indicate that US Army Africa took part in almost 80 percent of all AFRICOM activities on the continent in 2013, averaging more than one mission per day. Preliminary projections for 2014 suggested a similar pace—418 activities were already planned out by mid-December 2013—including anticipated increases in the number of operations and train-and-equip missions.

Full-scale exercises, each involving US Army troops and members of the militaries of multiple African countries, are also slated to rise from fourteen to twenty in 2014, according to the documents. So far, AFRICOM has released information on eleven named scheduled exercises. These include African Lion in Morocco, Eastern Accord in Uganda, Western Accord in Senegal, Central Accord in Cameroon, and Southern Accord in Malawi, all of which include a field training component and serve as a capstone event for the prior year's military-to-military programs. AFRICOM will also conduct at least three maritime security exercises, including Cutlass Express off the coast of East Africa, Obangame Express in the Gulf of Guinea, and Saharan Express in the waters off Senegal and the Cape Verde islands, as well as its annual Africa Endeavor exercise, which is designed to promote "information sharing" and facilitate standardized communications procedures within African militaries.

Additionally, US and African Special Operations forces will carry out an exercise codenamed Silent Warrior 2014 in Germany and have already completed Flintlock 2014, an annual event since 2005. As part of Flintlock 2014, more than one thousand troops from eighteen nations, including Burkina Faso, Canada, Chad, Denmark, France, Germany, Italy, Mauritania, the Netherlands, Nigeria, Norway, Senegal, the United Kingdom, the United States, and the host nation of Niger, carried out counterterror training on the outskirts of Niamey, the capital, as well as at small bases in Tahoua, Agadez, and Diffa. "Although Flintlock is considered an exercise, it is really an extension of ongoing training, engagement, and operations that help prepare our close Africa partners in the fight against extremism and the enemies that threaten peace, stability, and regional security," said Colonel Kenneth Sipperly, commander of the US Joint Special Operations Task Force-Trans Sahel, during the Flintlock opening ceremony.

Locations, Locations, Locations

A 2013 investigation by TomDispatch revealed that the US military was involved with at least forty-nine of the fifty-four nations on the African continent during 2012 and 2013. A map produced late last year by US Army Africa bolsters the findings, indicating its troops had conducted or planned to conduct "activities" in all African "countries" during the 2013 fiscal year except for Western Sahara (a disputed territory in the Maghreb region of North Africa), Guinea Bissau, Eritrea, Sudan, Somalia, São Tomé and Príncipe, Madagascar, and Zimbabwe. Egypt is considered outside of AFRICOM's area of operations, but did see U.S. military activity in 2013, as did Somalia, which now also hosts a small team of U.S. advisors. Other documents indicate army troops actually deployed to São Tomé and Príncipe, a country that regularly conducts activities with the US Navy.

We Know Not What They Do

"What We Are Doing," the title of a December 2013 military document obtained by TomDispatch, offers answers to questions that AFRICOM has long sought to avoid and provides information the command has worked to keep under wraps. So much else, however, remains in the shadows.

From 2008 to 2013, the number of missions, exercises, operations, and other activities under AFRICOM's purview skyrocketed from 172 to 546, but little substantive information was made public about what most of these missions involved and just whom US forces have trained. Since 2011, US Army Africa alone has taken part in close to one thousand "activities" across the continent. Independent reporters have only been on hand for a tiny fraction of them, so there are limits to what we can know about these missions beyond military talking points and official news releases for a relative few of them. Only later did it become clear that the United States extensively mentored the military officer who overthrew Mali's elected government in 2012, or that the United States had trained a Congolese commando battalion implicated by the United Nations in mass rapes and other atrocities that same year, to cite two examples.

Since its inception, US Africa Command has consistently downplayed its role on the continent. After years in the dark, however, we now know just how "extremely active"—to use General David Rodriguez's phrase—AFRICOM has been and how rapidly the tempo of its missions has increased. It remains to be seen just what else we don't know about US Africa Command's exponentially expanding operations.

6

AFRICOM Becomes a "War-Fighting Combatant Command": Going to War on the Sly

April 13, 2014

What the military will say to a reporter and what is said behind closed doors are two very different things—especially when it comes to the US military in Africa. At an April 2014 Pentagon press conference, for instance, AFRICOM Commander David Rodriguez adhered to the typical mantra, assuring reporters that the United States "has little forward presence" on that continent. Just days earlier, however, the men building the Pentagon's presence there were telling a very different story. They were, however, speaking in private to representatives of some of the biggest military engineering firms on the planet. They were planning for the future and the talk was of war.

I experienced this phenomenon myself during a media roundtable with Lieutenant General Thomas Bostick, commander of the

United States Army Corps of Engineers. When I asked the general to tell me just what his people were building for US forces in Africa, he paused and said in a low voice to the man next to him, "Can you help me out with that?" Lloyd Caldwell, the corps's director of military programs, whispered back, "Some of that would be close hold"—in other words, information too sensitive to reveal.

The only thing Bostick seemed eager to tell me about were vague plans to someday test a prototype "structural insulated panel-hut," a new energy-efficient type of barracks being developed by cadets at the US Military Academy at West Point. He also assured me that his people would get back to me with answers. What I got instead was an "interview" with a spokesman for the corps who offered little of substance when it came to construction on the African continent. Not much information was available, he said, the projects were tiny, only small amounts of money had been spent so far this year, much of it funneled into humanitarian efforts. In short, it seemed as if Africa was a construction backwater, a sleepy place, a vast landmass on which little of interest was happening.

Fast forward a few weeks to April 1, 2014 and Captain Rick Cook, the chief of US Africa Command's Engineer Division, was addressing an audience of more than fifty representatives of some of the largest military engineering firms on the planet—and this reporter. The contractors were interested in jobs and he wasn't pulling any punches. "The eighteen months or so that I've been here, we've been at war the whole time," Cook told them. "We are trying to provide opportunities for the African people to fix their own African challenges. Now, unfortunately, operations in Libya, South Sudan, and Mali, over the last two years, have proven there's always something going on in Africa."

Cook was one of three US military construction officials who, earlier this month, spoke candidly about the Pentagon's efforts in Africa to men and women from URS Corporation, AE-COM, CH2M Hill, and other top firms. During a paid-access web seminar, the three of them insisted that they were seeking industry "partners" because the military has "big plans" for the continent. They foretold a future marked by expansion, including the building up of a "permanent footprint" in Djibouti for the next decade or more, a possible new compound in Niger, and a string of bases devoted to surveillance activities spreading across the northern tier of Africa. They even let slip mention of a small, previously unacknowledged U.S. compound in Mali.

The Master Plan

After my brush-off by General Bostick, I interviewed an Army Corps of Engineers Africa expert, Chris Gatz, about construction projects for Special Operations Command Africa in 2013. "I'll be totally frank with you," he said, "as far as the scopes of these projects go, I don't have good insights."

What about two projects in Senegal I had stumbled across? Well, yes, he did, in fact, have information about a firing range and a "shoot house" that happened to be under construction there. When pressed, he also knew about plans I had noted in previously classified documents obtained by TomDispatch for the corps to build a multipurpose facility in Cameroon. And on we went. "You've got better information than I do," he said at one point, but it seemed like he had plenty of information, too. He just wasn't volunteering much of it to me.

Later, I asked if there were 2013 projects that had been funded with counter-narco-terrorism (CNT) money. "No, actually there was not," he told me. So I specifically asked about Niger.

Documents recently obtained by TomDispatch indicated

that the Army Corps of Engineers has been working on two CNT projects in Arlit and Tahoua, Niger. So I told Gatz what I had uncovered. Only then did he locate the right paperwork. "Oh, okay, I'm sorry," he replied. "You're right, we have two of them . . . Both were actually awarded to construction."

Those two CNT construction projects have been undertaken on behalf of Niger's security forces, but in his talk to construction industry representatives, AFRICOM's Rick Cook spoke about another project there: a possible US facility still to be built. "Lately, one of our biggest focus areas is in the country of Niger. We have gotten indications from the country of Niger that they are willing to be a partner of ours," he said. That nation, he added, "is in a nice strategic location that allows us to get to many other places reasonably quickly, so we are working very hard with the Nigerians to come up with, I wouldn't necessarily call it a base, but a place we can operate out of on a frequent basis."

Cook offered no information on the possible location of that facility, but contracting documents examined by TomDispatch indicate that the US Air Force is seeking to purchase large quantities of jet fuel to be delivered to Niger's Mano Dayak International Airport in Agadez.

Multiple requests for further information sent to media chief Benjamin Benson went unanswered, but Colonel Aaron Benson, chief of the Readiness Division at Air Forces Africa, did offer further details about the Nigerian mini-base. "There is the potential to construct MILCON aircraft parking aprons at the proposed future site in Niger," he wrote, mentioning a specific type of military construction funding dedicated to use for "enduring" bases rather than transitory facilities. In response to further questions, Cook referred to the possible site as a "base-like facility" that would be "semi-permanent" and "capable of air operations."

Pay to Play

It turns out that if you want to know what the US military is doing in Africa, it's advantageous to be connected to a large engineering or construction firm looking for business. Then you're privy to quite a different type of insider assessment of the future of the US presence there, one far more detailed than the modest official pronouncements that US Africa Command offers to journalists. Asked at a recent Pentagon press briefing if there were plans for a West African analog to Djibouti's Camp Lemonnier, the only "official" US base on the continent, General Rodriguez was typically guarded. Such a "forward-operating site" was just "one of the options" the command was mulling over, he said, before launching into the sort of fuzzy language typical of official answers. "What we're really looking at doing is putting contingency locating sites, which really have some just expeditionary infrastructure that can be expanded with tents," was the way he put it. He never once mentioned Niger, or airfield improvements, or the possibility of a semi-permanent "presence."

Here, however, is the reality as we know it today. Over the past several years, the United States has been building a constellation of drone bases across Africa, flying intelligence, surveillance, and reconnaissance missions out of not only Niger, but also Djibouti, Ethiopia, and the island nation of the Seychelles. Meanwhile, an airbase in Ouagadougou, the capital of Burkina Faso, serves as the home of a Joint Special Operations Air Detachment, as well as of the Trans-Sahara Short Take-Off and Landing Airlift Support initiative. According to military documents, that "initiative" supports "high-risk activities" carried out by elite forces from Joint Special Operations Task Force-Trans Sahara.

As part of the webinar for industry representatives, Wayne Uhl, chief of the International Engineering Center for the Europe Dis-

US facility near Gao, Mali. This austere compound is thought to have been overrun by Islamist forces in 2012. Credit: US Army Corps of Engineers.

trict of the Army Corps of Engineers, shed light on shadowy US operations in Mali before (and possibly after) the elected government there was overthrown in 2012. Documents prepared by Uhl reveal that an American compound was constructed near Gao, a major city in the north of Mali. Gao is the site of multiple Malian military bases and a "strategic" airport captured by Islamist militants in 2012 and retaken by French and Malian troops early last year.

AFRICOM's Benson failed to respond to multiple requests for comment about the Gao compound, but Uhl offered additional details. The project was completed before the 2012 uprising and "included a vehicle maintenance facility, a small admin building, toilet facilities with water tank, a diesel generator with a fuel storage tank, and a perimeter fence," he told me in a written response to my questions. "I imagine the site was overrun during the coup and is no longer used by U.S. forces."

Meanwhile America's lone official base, Camp Lemonnier, a former French Foreign Legion post, has been on a decade-plus growth spurt and serves a key role for the US mission. "Camp Lemonnier is the only permanent footprint that we have on the continent and until such time as AFRICOM may establish a headquarters location in Africa, Camp Lemonnier will be the center of their activities here," Greg Wilderman, the Military Construction Program manager for Naval Facilities Engineering Command, explained.

"In 2013, we had a big jump in the amount of program projects," he noted, specifically mentioning a large "task force" construction effort, an oblique reference to a $220 million Special Operations compound at the base that TomDispatch first reported on in 2013.

According to documents provided by Wilderman, five contracts worth more than $322 million (to be paid via MILCON funds) were awarded for Camp Lemonnier in late 2013. These included deals for a $25.5 million fitness center and a $41 million Joint Headquarters Facility in addition to the Special Operations Compound. In 2014, Wilderman noted, there are two contracts—valued at $35 million— already slated to be awarded, and Captain Rick Cook specifically mentioned deals for an armory and new barracks.

Cook's presentation also indicated that a number of long-running construction projects at Camp Lemonnier were set to be completed this year, including roads, a "fuel farm," an aircraft logistics apron, and "taxiway enhancements," while construction of a new aircraft maintenance hangar, a telecommunications facility, and a "combat aircraft loading area" are slated to be finished in 2015. "There's a tremendous amount of work going on," Cook said, noting that there were twenty-two current projects under way there, more than at any other navy base anywhere in the world.

And this, it turns out, is only the beginning.

"In the master plan," Cook said, "there is close to three quarters of a billion dollars worth of construction projects that we still would like to do at Camp Lemonnier over the next ten to fifteen years." That base, in turn, would be just one of a constellation of camps and compounds used by the United States in Africa.

"Many of the places that we are trying to stand up or trying to get into are air missions. A lot of ISR [intelligence, surveillance, and reconnaissance] . . . is going on in different parts of the continent. Generally speaking, the air force is probably going to be assigned to do much of that," he told the contractors. "The air force is going to be doing a great deal of work on these bases . . . that are going to be built across the northern tier of Africa."

Hearts and Minds

When I spoke with Chris Gatz of the Army Corps of Engineers, the first projects he mentioned and the only ones he seemed eager to talk about were those for African nations. In 2014, $6.5 million in projects had been funded when we spoke and of that, the majority were for "humanitarian assistance" (HA) construction projects, mostly in Togo and Tunisia, and "peacekeeping" operations in Ghana and Djibouti.

Uhl talked about humanitarian projects, too. "HA projects are small, difficult, challenging for the Corps of Engineers to accomplish at a low, in-house cost . . . but despite all this, HA projects are extremely rewarding," he said. "The appreciation expressed by the locals is fantastic." He then drew attention to another added benefit: "Each successful project is a photo opportunity."

Uhl wasn't the only official to touch on the importance of public perception in Africa or the need to curry favor with military "partners" on the continent. Cook spoke to the contractors, for instance, about the challenges of work in austere locations, about how bureaucratic shakedowns by members of African governments could cause consternation and construction delays, about learning to work with the locals, and about how important such efforts were for "winning hearts and minds of folks in the area."

The Naval Facilities Engineering Command's Wilderman talked up the challenges of working in an environment in which the availability of resources was limited, the dangers of terrorism were real, and there was "competition for cooperation with [African] countries from some other world powers." This was no doubt a reference to increasing Chinese trade, aid, investment, and economic ties across the continent.

He also left no doubt about US plans. "We will be in Africa for some time to come," he told the contractors. "There's lots more to do there."

Cook expanded on this theme. "It's a big, big place," he said. "We know we can't do it alone. So we're going to need partners in industry, we're going to need . . . local nationals and even third-country nationals."

AFRICOM at War

AFRICOM'S public persona remains one of humanitarian missions and benign-sounding support for local partners. "Our core mission of assisting African states and regional organizations to strengthen their defense capabilities better enables Africans to address their security threats and reduces threats to U.S. interests," says the command. "We concentrate our efforts on contributing to the development of capable and professional militaries that respect human rights, adhere to the rule of law, and more effectively contribute to stability in Africa." Efforts like sniper training for proxy forces and black ops missions hardly come up. Bases are mostly ignored. The word *war* is rarely mentioned.

TomDispatch's recent investigations have, however, revealed that the US military is indeed pivoting to Africa. It now averages far more than a mission a day on the continent, conducting operations with almost every African military force, in almost every African country, while building or building up camps, compounds, and "contingency security locations." The United States has taken an active role in wars from Libya to the Central African Republic, sent special ops forces into countries from Somalia to South Sudan, conducted airstrikes and abduction missions, even put boots on the ground in countries where it pledged it would not.

"We have shifted from our original intent of being a more congenial combatant command to an actual war-fighting combatant command," AFRICOM's Rick Cook explained to the audience of big-money defense contractors. He was unequivocal: the United States has been "at war" on the continent for the last two and half years. It remains to be seen when AFRICOM will pass this news on to the American public.

7

The Pentagon, Libya, and Tomorrow's Blowback Today: How Not to End Violence in a War-Torn Land

April 15, 2014

Is the United States secretly training Libyan militiamen in the Canary Islands? And if not, are they planning to?

That's what I asked a spokesman for US Africa Command (AFRICOM). "I am surprised by your mentioning the Canary Islands," he responded by email. "I have not heard this before, and wonder where you heard this."

As it happens, mention of this shadowy mission on the Spanish archipelago off the northwest coast of Africa was revealed in an official briefing prepared for AFRICOM chief David Rodriguez in the fall of 2013. In the months after, the plan may have been permanently shelved in favor of a training mission carried out entirely in Bulgaria. The document nonetheless highlights the US military's penchant for simple solutions to complex problems—with a well-documented potential for blowback in Africa and beyond. It also raises serious questions about the recurring methods employed by the United States to stop the violence its actions helped spark in the first place.

Ever since the United States helped oust dictator Muammar Gaddafi, with air and missile strikes against regime targets and major logistical and surveillance support to coalition partners, Libya has been sliding into increasing chaos. Militias, some of them jihadist, have sprung up across the country, carving out fiefdoms while carrying out increasing numbers of assassinations and other types of attacks. The solution seized upon by the United States and its allies in response to the devolving situation there: introduce yet another armed group into a country already rife with them.

The Rise of the Militias

After Gaddafi's fall in 2011, a wide range of militias came to dominate Libya's largest cities, filling a security vacuum left by the collapse of the old regime and providing a challenge to the new central government. In Benghazi alone, an array of these armed groups arose. And on September 11, 2012, that city, considered the cradle of the Libyan revolution, experienced attacks by members of the anti-Western Ansar al-Sharia, as well as other militias on the American mission and a nearby CIA facility. During those assaults, which killed Ambassador J. Christopher Stevens and three other Americans, local armed groups called on for help or which might have intervened to save lives reportedly stood aside.

Over the year that followed, the influence of the militias only continued to grow nationwide, as did the chaos that accompanied them. In late 2013, following deadly attacks on civilians, some of these forces were chased from Libyan cities by protestors and armed bands, ceding power to what the *New York Times* called "an even more fractious collection of armed groups, including militias representing tribal and clan allegiances that tear at the tenuous [Libyan] sense of common citizenship." With the situation deteriorating, the humanitarian group Human Rights Watch documented dozens of assassinations of judges, prosecutors, and members of the state's already weakened security forces by unidentified assailants.

The American solution to all of this violence: more armed men.

Fighting Fire with Fire

In November 2013, US Special Operations Command Chief Admiral William McRaven told an audience at the Ronald Reagan Presidential Library that the United States would aid Libya by training 5,000 to 7,000 conventional troops as well as counterterrorism forces there. "As we go forward to try and find a good way to build up the Libyan security forces so they are not run by militias, we are going to have to assume some risks," he said.

Not long after, the *Washington Post* reported a request by recently ousted Libyan prime minister Ali Zeidan that the United States train his country's security forces. In January, the Pentagon's Defense Security Cooperation Agency, which coordinates sales and transfers of military equipment abroad, formally notified Congress of a Libyan request for a $600 million training package. Its goal: to create a 6,000–8,000-man "general purpose force," or GPF.

The deal would, according to an official statement, involve "services for up to 8 years for training, facilities sustainment and improvements, personnel training and training equipment, 637 M4A4 carbines and small arms ammunition, U.S. Government and contractor technical and logistics support services, Organizational Clothing and Individual Equipment (OCIE), and other related elements of logistical and program support."

In addition to the GPF effort, thousands of Libyan troops are to be trained by the militaries of Morocco, Turkey, the United Kingdom, and Italy. The Libyan Army also hopes to graduate 10,000 new troops at home annually.

While Admiral McRaven has emphasized the importance of building up "the Libyan security forces so they are not run by militias," many recruits for the GPF will, in fact, be drawn from these very groups. It has also been widely reported that the new force will be trained at Novo Selo, a recently refurbished facility in Bulgaria.

The United States has said little else of substance on the future force. "We are coordinating this training mission closely with our European partners and the U.N. Support Mission in Libya, who have also offered substantial security sector assistance to the Government of Libya," a State Department official told TomDispatch by email. "We expect this training will begin in 2014 in Bulgaria and continue over a number of years."

There have been no reports or confirmation of the plan to also train Libyan militiamen at a facility in Spain's Canary Islands mentioned along with Novo Selo in that fall 2013 briefing document prepared for General Rodriguez, which was obtained by TomDispatch.

Officials at the State Department say that they know nothing about this part of the program. "I'm still looking into this, but my colleagues are not familiar with a Canary Islands component to this issue," I was told by a State Department press officer.

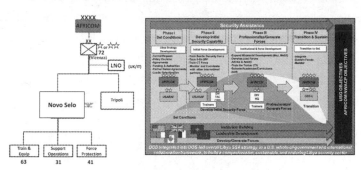

- Mission Command element OPCON to AFRICOM and based in Vicenza, Italy
- LNOs to Partner Training missions in UK, IT, and TU
- Tripoli, Libya includes Train/Equip, Screening, JRSOI teams and Embassy Liaison
- Two Training Elements (Novo Selo & Canary Islands)
- Training Elements include Trainers, Force Protection, and Support elements

21-Jan-14   UNCLASSIFIED   13

Official briefing slide mentioning a US military training effort in the Canary Islands.

AFRICOM spokesman Benson said much the same. "We have no information regarding training of Libyan troops to be provided in the Canary Islands," he emailed me. After I sent him the briefing slide that mentioned the mission, however, he had a different response. The Canary Islands training mission was, he wrote, part of an "initial concept" never actually shared with General Rodriguez, but instead "briefed to a few senior leaders in the Pentagon."

"The information has been changed, numerous times, since the slide was drafted, and is expected to change further before any training commences," he added, and warned me against relying on it. He did not, however, rule out the possibility that further changes might revive the Canary Islands option and demurred from answering further questions on the subject. A separate US Army Africa document does mention that "recon" of a second training site was slated to begin last December.

Neither the State Department nor AFRICOM explained why plans to conduct training in the Canary Islands were shelved or when that decision was made or by whom. Benson also failed to facilitate interviews with personnel involved in the Libyan GPF training effort or with top AFRICOM commanders. "Given the continuing developing nature of this effort, it would be inappropriate to comment further at this time, and we have not been giving interviews on the topic," he told me. Multiple requests to the Libyan government for information on the locations of training sites also went unanswered.

Training Day

Wherever the training takes place, the United States has developed a four-phase process to "build a complete Libya security sector." The Army's 1st Infantry Division will serve as the "mission command element for the Libyan GPF training effort" as part of a State Department–led collaboration with the Department of Defense, according to official documents obtained by TomDispatch.

Agreements with partner nations are to be finalized and Libyans selected for leadership positions as part of an initial stage of the process. Then the US military will begin training not only the GPF troops but a border security force and specialized counterterror troops. (General Rodriguez told the Senate Armed Services Committee that the United States was also helping build up what he called Libyan "Special Operations Forces.") A third phase of the program will involve developing the capacities of the Libyan ministries of justice, defense, and the interior, and strengthening Libya's homegrown security training apparatus, before pulling back during a fourth phase that will focus on monitoring and sustaining the forces the United States and its allies have trained.

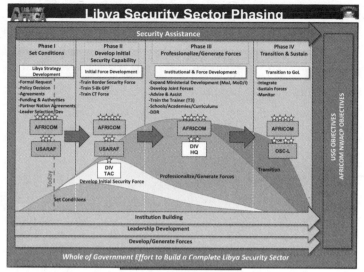

US Army Africa document details four-phase plan for US training of Libyan forces.

Despite reports that training at Novo Selo were to begin in the spring of 2014, a State Department official told TomDispatch that detailed plans are still being finalized. After inspecting a briefing slide titled "Libya Security Sector Phasing," Benson told me, "I do not see us in any phase as indicated on the slide . . . the planning and coordination is still ongoing." Lolita Baldor of the Associated Press reported that, according to an unnamed army official, a small team of US soldiers has headed for Libya to make preparations for the Bulgarian portion of the training.

A timeline produced by US Army Africa as part of a December 2013 briefing indicated that the Novo Selo site would be ready for trainers by March 2014, but in April General Rodriguez pointed out at a Pentagon press briefing that the Libyan government had yet to ante up the funds for the program, and a Libyan official confirmed to TomDispatch that the training had yet to commence.

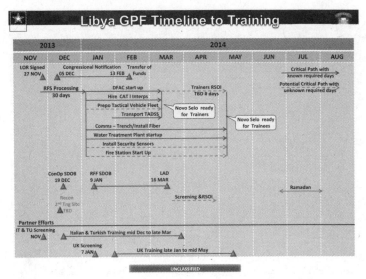

US Army Africa timeline of US training of Libyan General Purpose Force.

Experts have, however, already expressed skepticism about the effectiveness of the program. In late 2013, for instance, Benjamin Nickels, the academic chair for transnational threats and counterterrorism at the Department of Defense's Africa Center for Strategic Studies, raised a number of problematic issues. These included the challenge of screening and vetting applicants from existing Libyan militias, the difficulty of incorporating various regional and tribal groups into such a force without politicizing the trainee pool, and the daunting task of then devising a way to integrate the GPF into Libya's existing military in a situation already verging on the chaotic.

"For all their seriousness," wrote Nickels, "these implementation difficulties pale in comparison to more serious pitfalls haunting the GPF at a conceptual level. So far, plans for the GPF appear virtually unrelated to projects of disarmament, demobilization, and reintegration (DDR) and security sector reform (SSR) that are vital to Libya's future."

Berny Sebe, an expert on North and West Africa at the University of Birmingham in the United Kingdom, noted that, while incorporating militiamen into a "mainstream security system" could help diminish the power of existing militias, it posed serious dangers as well. "The drawback is, of course, that it can infiltrate factious elements into the very heart of the Libyan state apparatus, which could further undermine its power," he told TomDispatch by email. "The use of force is unavoidable to enforce the rule of law, which is regularly under threat in Libya. However, all efforts placed in the development of a security force should go hand in hand with a clear political vision. Failure to do so might solve the problem temporarily, but will not bring long-term peace and stability."

In November 2013, Frederic Wehrey, a senior associate with the Carnegie Endowment for International Peace and an expert on Libya, pointed out that the project seemed reasonable in the abstract, but reality might be another matter entirely: "The force's composition, the details of its training, the extent to which Libyan civilians will oversee it, and its ability to deal with the range of threats that the country faces are all unclear." He suggested that an underreported 2013 mission to train one Libyan unit that ended in abject failure should be viewed as a cautionary tale.

In the summer of 2013, a small contingent of US Special Operations forces set up a training camp outside of Libya's capital, Tripoli, for an elite 100-man Libyan counterterror force whose recruits were personally chosen by former Prime Minister Ali Zeidan. While the Americans were holed up in their nighttime safe house, unidentified militia or "terrorist" forces twice raided the camp, guarded by the Libyan military, and looted large quantities of high-tech American equipment. Their haul included hundreds of weapons, Glock pistols and M4 rifles among them, as well as night-vision devices and specialized lasers that can only be seen with such equipment. As a result, the training effort was shut down and the abandoned camp was reportedly taken over by a militia.

This represented only the latest in a series of troubled US assistance and training efforts in the greater Middle East and Africa. These include scandal-plagued endeavors in Iraq and Afghanistan, as well as a program that produced an officer who led the coup that overthrew Mali's elected government. These are just the tip of the iceberg among many other sordid examples from around the world.

The Answer?

The United States may never train a single Libyan militiaman in the Canary Islands, but the plan to create yet one more armed group to inject into Libya's already fractious sea of competing militias is fraught with peril.

For more than half a year, a militia controlled the three largest ports in Libya. Other militiamen have killed unarmed protestors. Some have emptied whole towns of their residents. Others work with criminal gangs, smuggling drugs, carrying out kidnappings for ransom, and engaging in human trafficking. Still others have carried out arbitrary arrests, conducted torture, and been responsible for deaths in detention. Armed men have also murdered foreigners, targeted Christian migrants, and fought pro-government forces. Many have attacked other nascent state institutions. In March 2014, for instance, militiamen stormed the country's national assembly, forcing its relocation to a hotel. (That assault was apparently triggered by a separate unidentified group, which attacked an anti-parliament sit-in, kidnapping some of the protestors.)

Some militias have quasi-official status or are beholden to individual parliamentarians. Others are paid by and support the rickety Libyan government. That government is also reportedly engaging in widespread abuses, including detentions without due process and prosecutions to stifle free speech, while failing to repeal Gaddafi-era laws that, as Human Rights Watch has noted, "prescribe corporal punishment, including lashing for extramarital intercourse and slander, and amputation of limbs."

Most experts agree that Libya needs assistance in strengthening its central government and the rule of law. "Unless the international community focuses on the need for urgent assistance to the justice and security systems, Libya risks the collapse of its already weak state institutions and further deterioration of human rights in the country," Sarah Leah Whitson, Middle East and North Africa director at Human Rights Watch, has typically said. How to go about this remains, however, at best unclear.

"Our Defense Department colleagues plan to train 5,000 to 8,000 general purpose forces," Anne Patterson, the assistant secretary of state for Near Eastern Affairs, told the House Armed Services Committee, noting that the United States would "conduct an unprecedented vetting and screening of trainees that participate in the program." But Admiral William McRaven, her "Defense Department colleague," has already admitted that some of the troops to be trained will likely not have "the most clean record."

In the wake of failed full-scale conflicts in Iraq and Afghanistan, the US military has embraced a light-footprint model of warfare, emphasizing drone technology, Special Operations forces, and above all the training of proxy troops to fight battles for America's national security interests from Mali to Syria—and now Libya as well.

There are, of course, no easy answers. As Berny Sebe notes, the United States "is among the few countries in the world which have the resources necessary to undertake such a gigantic task as training the new security force of a country on the brink of civil war like Libya." Yet the United States has repeatedly suffered from poor intelligence, an inability to deal effectively with the local and regional dynamics involved in operations in the Middle East and North Africa, and massive doses of wishful thinking and poor planning. "It is indeed a dangerous decision," Sebe observes, "which may add further confusion to an already volatile situation."

A failure to imagine the consequences of the last major US intervention in Libya has perhaps irreparably fractured the country and sent it into a spiral of violence leading to the deaths of Americans, among others, while helping destabilize neighboring nations, enhance the reach of local terror groups, and aid in the proliferation of weapons that have fueled existing regional conflicts. Even deputy assistant secretary of defense for African Affairs Amanda Dory admitted at a recent Pentagon press briefing that the fallout from ousting Gaddafi has been "worse than would have been anticipated at the time." Perhaps it should be sobering as well that the initial smaller scale effort to help strengthen Libyan security forces was an abject failure that ended up enhancing, not diminishing, the power of the militias.

There may be no nation that can get things entirely right when it comes to Libya, but one nation has shown an unnerving ability to get things wrong. Whether outside of Tripoli, in Bulgaria, the Canary Islands, or elsewhere, should that country really be the one in charge of the delicate process of building a cohesive security force to combat violent, fractious armed groups? Should it really be creating a separate force, trained far from home by foreigners, and drawn from the very militias that have destabilized Libya in the first place?

Update: November 2014

The situation in Libya only continued to deteriorate. By late 2014, the country found itself engulfed in militia violence, with ever more Libyans dead, wounded, or displaced and two rival parliaments and governments battling for control of a near-failed state.

Plans to train Libyan forces abroad also crashed and burned. The British effort immediately imploded as one-third of the carefully vetted recruits were "withdrawn" for various reasons. Some left because of disciplinary issues, some for personal and medical reasons; others were found to be uninterested in the training. Worse yet, five Libyan officers were charged with committing sex offenses, including rape, in and around the city of Cambridge. The entire initial cohort of 300 Libyans were finally sent home and the program suspended.

An Italian program officially trained 1,320 soldiers in Libya and 185 in Italy, but upon graduation, many reportedly joined militias, not the Libyan military.

The US effort to create the General Purpose Force was an even more resounding failure than the European schemes. It never trained a single soldier. In fact, the effort never even began.

Not surprisingly, no one is particularly interested in talking about any of this. When I arrived for a long-scheduled meeting to discuss GPF training with Colonel Ibrahim Elfurtia, the Libyan defense attaché in Washington, DC, I was told that he had unexpectedly left for his homeland that morning and no one else could speak with me. When I sought an update from the State Department in November 2014, an official, who asked that I not use his name, would offer only the most cursory of comments that nonetheless spoke volumes: "Our GPF training program is necessarily being delayed as we reevaluate how to effectively work with the Libyans to advance this effort in light of the current situation on the ground." Grounded, in other words, by the "situation on the ground."

8

How "Benghazi" Birthed the New Normal in Africa: A Secret African Mission and an African Mission That's No Secret

May 15, 2014

What is Operation New Normal?

It's a question without an answer, a riddle the US military refuses to solve. It's a secret operation in Africa that no one knows anything about. Except that someone does. His name is Lieutenant Colonel Robert E. Lee Magee. He lives and breathes Operation New Normal. But he doesn't want to breathe paint fumes or talk to me, so you can't know anything about it.

Confused? Stay with me on this one.

Whatever Operation New Normal may be pales in comparison to the real "new normal" for US Africa Command. The lowercased variant is bold and muscular. It's an expeditionary force on a war footing. To the men involved, it's a story of growth and expansion, new battlefields, "combat," and "war." It's the culmination of years of construction, ingratiation, and interventions, the fruits of wide-eyed expansion and dismal policy failures, the backing of proxies to fight America's battles, while increasing US personnel and firepower in and around the continent. It is, to quote an officer with AFRICOM, the blossoming of a "war-fighting combatant command." And unlike Operation New Normal, it's finally heading for a media outlet near you.

Ever Less New, Ever More Normal

With the end of the Iraq War and the drawdown of combat forces in Afghanistan, Washington has, however, visibly "pivoted" to Africa and, for the first time in years in late spring 2014, many news organizations, especially those devoted to the military, began waking up to the new normal there and actually report on it from time to time.

While daily US troop strength continent-wide hovers in the relatively modest range of 5,000 to 8,000 personnel, an under-the-radar expansion has been constant. This increased engagement has come at a continuing cost. When the United States and other allies intervened in 2011 to aid in the ouster of Libyan dictator Muammar Gaddafi, for instance, it helped set off a chain reaction that led to a security vacuum destabilizing that country as well as neighboring Mali. Libya has not recovered and has been tottering toward failed-state status ever since.

Meanwhile, quickly politicized by congressional Republicans and conservative news outlets, the word *Benghazi* has become a shorthand for many things, including Obama administration cover-ups and misconduct, as well as White House lies and malfeasance. Missing, however, has been thoughtful analysis of the implications of American power projection in Africa or the possibility that blowback might result from it.

Far from being chastened by the Benghazi deaths or chalking them up to a failure to imagine the consequences of armed interventions in situations whose local politics they barely grasp, the Pentagon and the Obama administration have used Benghazi as a growth opportunity, a means to take military efforts on the continent to the next level. "Benghazi" has provided AFRICOM with a beefed-up mandate and new clout. It birthed the new normal in Africa.

The Spoils of Blowback

The 2012 killings of an American ambassador and three other Americans "changed AFRICOM forever," Major General Raymond Fox, commander of the II Marine Expeditionary Force, told attendees of a Sea-Air-Space conference organized by the Navy League, the Marine Corps, the Coast Guard, and the Merchant Marine. The proof lies in the new "crisis response" forces that have popped up in and around Africa, greatly enhancing the regional reach, capabilities, and firepower of the US military.

Following the debacle in Benghazi, for instance, the United States established an Africa-focused force known as Special-Purpose Marine Air-Ground Task Force-Crisis Response (SP-MAGTF CR) to give AFRICOM quick-reaction capabilities on the continent. "Temporarily positioned" at Morón Air Base in Spain, this rotating unit of marines and sailors is officially billed as "a balanced, expeditionary force with built-in command, ground, aviation, and logistics elements and organized, trained, and equipped to accomplish a specific mission."

Similarly, Benghazi provided the justification for the birthing of another rapid reaction unit, the Commander's In-Extremis Force. Long in the planning stages and supported by the head of the Special Operations Command, Admiral McRaven, the Fort Carson, Colorado–based unit—part of the 10th Special Forces Group—was sent to Europe weeks after Benghazi. Elements of this specialized counterterrorism unit are now "constantly forward deployed," AFRICOM's Benson told TomDispatch, and stand "ready for the commander to use, if there's a crisis."

The East Africa Response Force (EARF), operating from Camp Lemonnier in Djibouti, is another new quick-reaction unit. When asked about EARF, Benson said, "The growing complexity of the security environment demonstrated the need for us to have a [Department of Defense]-positioned response force that could respond to crises in the African region."

In late December 2013, just days after the 1st Combined Arms Battalion, 18th Infantry Regiment, out of Fort Riley, Kansas, arrived in Djibouti to serve as the newly christened EARF, members of the unit were whisked off to South Sudan. Led by EARF's commander, Lieutenant Colonel Lee Magee, the forty-five-man platoon was dispatched to that restive nation (fostered into being by the United States only a few years earlier) as it slid toward civil war with armed factions moving close to the US embassy in the capital, Juba. The obvious fear: another Benghazi.

Joined by elements of the SP-MAGTF CR and more shadowy special ops troops, members of EARF helped secure and reinforce the embassy and evacuate Americans. Magee and most of his troops returned to Djibouti in February, although a few remained in South Sudan until at least April.

A nation the United States poured much time and effort into building, South Sudan was at the time lurching toward the brink of genocide, according to Secretary of State John Kerry. With a ceasefire already in shambles within hours of being signed, the country stood as yet another stark foreign policy failure on a continent now rife with them. But just as Benghazi proved a useful excuse for dispatching more forward-deployed firepower toward Africa, the embassy scare in South Sudan acted as a convenient template for future crises in which the US military would be even more involved. "We're basically the firemen for AFRICOM. If something arises and they need troops somewhere, we can be there just like that," Captain John Young, a company commander with the East Africa Response Force, told *Stars and Stripes* in the wake of the Juba mission.

The New Normal and the Same Old, Same Old

A batch of official Army Africa documents obtained by TomDispatch convinced me that EARF was intimately connected with Operation New Normal. A July 2013 briefing slide, for instance, references "East Africa Response Force/New Normal," while another concerning operations on that continent mentions "New Normal Reaction Force East." At the same time, the phrase "new normal" has been increasingly on the lips of the men running America's African ops.

Jason Hyland, a thirty-year State Department veteran who serves as foreign policy advisor to Brigadier General Wayne Grigsby, the commander of Combined Joint Task Force–Horn of Africa (CJTF-HOA), for instance, told an interviewer that the task force "is at the forefront in this region in implementing U.S. policy on the 'new normal' to protect our missions when there are uncertain conditions."

A news release from CJTF-HOA concerning the Juba operation also used the phrase: "While the East Africa Response Force was providing security for the embassy, additional forces were required to continue the evacuation mission. Under the auspices of 'the new normal,' which refers to the heightened threat U.S. Embassies face throughout the world, the SP-MAGTF CR arrived from Morón, Spain," wrote Technical Sergeant Jasmine Reif.

In *Seapower* magazine, the commander of SP-MAGTF CR, Colonel Scott Benedict, described the "new normal" as a world filled with "a lot of rapidly moving crises," requiring military interventions and likened it to the Marine Corps deployments in the so-called Banana Wars in Central America and the Caribbean in the early twentieth century.

On a visit to Camp Lemonnier, marine commandant General James Amos echoed the same sentiments, calling his troops "America's insurance policy." Referencing the marine task force, he invoked that phrase in an even more expansive way. Aside from "winning battles" in Afghanistan, he said, the creation of that force was "probably the most significant thing we've done in the last year and a half as far as adjusting the Marine Corps for what people are now calling the new normal, which are these crises that are happening around the world."

In March, Brigadier General Grigsby explicitly noted that the phrase meant far more than simple embassy security missions. "Sitting in Djibouti is really the new normal," the CJTF-HOA commander said. (And he was, in fact, sitting in an office in that country.) "It's not the new normal . . . as far as providing security for our threatened embassies. It's really the new normal on how we're going to operate as a [Department of Defense entity] in supporting the national security strategy of our country."

Operation New Normal and
the Incredible Disappearing Lee Magee

With so many officials talking about the "new normal" and with documents citing a specific operation sporting the same name, I once again called up Benjamin Benson looking for more information. "I don't know the name new normal," he told me. "It isn't a term we're using to define one of the operations."

That seemed curious. An official military document obtained by TomDispatch explicitly noted that US troops would be deployed as part of Operation New Normal in 2014. The term was even used, in still another document, alongside other code-named operations like Juniper Micron and Observant Compass, missions to aid the French and African interventions in Mali and to degrade or destroy Joseph Kony's murderous Lord's Resistance Army in central Africa.

Next I got in touch with Lieutenant Colonel Glen Roberts at CJTF-HOA and explained that I wanted to know about Operation New Normal. His response was effusive and unequivocal: I should speak with Lee Magee—that is, Lieutenant Colonel Robert E. Lee Magee, third-generation army officer, West Point graduate, and commander of the East African Response Force who had deployed to South Sudan as that nation shattered on the rocks of reality. "He lives this concept and has executed it," was how Roberts put it.

Was I available to talk to Magee the next day? Yes, indeed I was.

On March 27, the day of the proposed interview, however, a lower-ranking public affairs official got in touch to explain that Lieutenant Colonel Magee could not speak to me and Lieutenant Colonel Roberts was out of the office. I asked to reschedule for the next day. The spokesman said he didn't know what their cal-

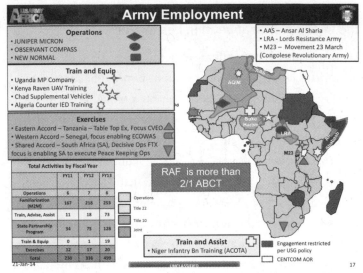

From a 2013 US Army Africa briefing slide referencing
Operation New Normal.

endars looked like, but that Roberts was expected back later that day. I left a message, but heard nothing.

The next morning, I called the press office in Djibouti and asked to speak to Magee. He wasn't there. No one was. Everyone had left work early. The reason? "Paint fumes."

That was a new one.

Another follow-up and Roberts finally got back in touch. "Apologies, but I am no longer able to arrange an interview with Magee," he informed me. "Thanks for understanding."

But I didn't understand and told him so. After all, Magee was the man who *lived and executed* the new normal. I thought we were set for an interview. What happened?

"He has simply declined an interview, as is his privilege," was the best Roberts could do. Magee had been dropped into the hot zone in South Sudan to forestall the next Benghazi and had previously spoken with other media outlets about his work in Africa, but conversing with me about Operation New Normal was apparently beyond the pale. Or maybe it had something to do with those paint fumes.

On March 31, Roberts told me that he could answer the questions by email—questions that I had already sent in on March 17. But no response came. I followed up again. And again. And again. I sent the questions a second time.

Almost two months after my initial inquiry, no word had come and it never has. That, evidently, is the new normal, too.

The Real New Normal

Obviously the U.S. military isn't eager to talk about Operation New Normal, which—despite Benson's contentions, Magee's silence, and Roberts's disappearance—is almost certainly the name for a US military mission in East Africa that, US documents suggest, is tied to the Benghazi-birthed East African Response Force (EARF).

More important than uncovering the nature of Operation New Normal, however, is recognizing the real new normal in Africa for the US military: ever-increasing missions across the continent, ever more engagement with local proxies in ever more African countries, the construction of more new facilities in ever more countries, and a string of bases devoted to surveillance activities spreading across the northern tier of the continent. Add to this impressive buildup the three new rapid reaction forces, specialized teams like a contingent of AFRICOM personnel and officials from the FBI and the departments of Justice, State, and Defense created to help rescue hundreds of Nigerian schoolgirls kidnapped by members of the Islamic militant group Boko Haram, and other shadowy quick-response units like the seldom-mentioned Naval Special Warfare Unit 10.

"Having resources [on the continent] that are ready for a response is really valuable," Benson told me when talking about the Djibouti-based EARF. The same holds for the US military's new normal in Africa: more of everything valuable to a military seeking a new mission in the wake of two fading, none-too-successful wars.

The Benghazi killings, unrest in South Sudan, and the Boko Haram kidnappings have provided the United States with ways to bring a long-running "light footprint in Africa" narrative into line with a far heavier reality. Each crisis has provided the US with further justification for publicizing a steady expansion on that continent that's been under way but under wraps for years. New forces, new battlefields, and a new openness about a new "war," to quote one of the men waging it. That's the real new normal for the US military in Africa—and you don't need to talk to Lieutenant Colonel Lee Magee to know it.

9

An East-West Showdown: China, America, and a New Cold War in Africa?

July 31, 2014

JUBA, South Sudan. Is this country the first hot battlefield in a new cold war? Is the conflict tearing this new nation apart actually a proxy fight between the world's top two economic and military powers? That's the way South Sudan's information minister Michael Makuei Lueth tells it. After "midwifing" South Sudan into existence with billions of dollars in assistance, aid, infrastructure projects, and military support, the United States has watched China emerge as the major beneficiary of South Sudan's oil reserves. As a result, Makuei claims, the United States and other Western powers have backed former Vice President Riek Machar and his rebel forces in an effort to overthrow the country's president, Salva Kiir. China, for its part, has played a conspicuous double game. Beijing has lined up behind Kiir, even as it publicly pushes both sides to find a diplomatic solution to a simmering civil war. It is sending peacekeepers as part of a UN mission even as it also arms Kiir's forces with tens of millions of dollars' worth of new weapons.

While experts dismiss Makuei's scenario—"farfetched" is how one analyst puts it—there are average South Sudanese who also believe that Washington supports the rebels. The United States certainly did press Kiir's government to make concessions, as his supporters are quick to remind anyone willing to listen, pushing it to release senior political figures detained as coup plotters shortly after fighting broke out in late 2013. America, they say, cared more about a handful of elites sitting in jail than all the South Sudanese suffering in a civil war that has now claimed more than 10,000 lives, resulted in mass rapes, displaced more than 1.5 million people (around half of them children), and pushed the country to the very brink of famine. Opponents of Kiir are, however, quick to mention the significant quantities of Chinese weaponry flooding into the country. They ask why the United States hasn't put pressure on a president they no longer see as legitimate.

While few outside South Sudan would ascribe to Makuei's notion of a direct east-west proxy war here, his conspiracy theory should at least serve as a reminder that US and Chinese interests are at play in this war-torn nation and across Africa as a whole—and that Africans are taking note. Almost anywhere you look on the continent, you can now find evidence of both the American and the Chinese presence, although they take quite different forms. The Chinese are pursuing a ruthlessly pragmatic economic power-projection strategy with an emphasis on targeted multilateral interventions in African conflict zones. US policy, in contrast, appears both more muddled and more military-centric, with a heavy focus on counterterrorism efforts meant to bolster amorphous strategic interests.

For the past decade, China has used "soft power"—aid, trade, and infrastructure projects—to make major inroads on the continent. In the process, it has set itself up as the dominant foreign player here. The United States, on the other hand, increasingly confronts Africa as a "battlefield" or "battleground" or "war" in the words of the men running its operations. In recent years, there has been a substantial surge in US military activities of every sort, including the setting up of military outposts and both direct and proxy interventions. These two approaches have produced starkly contrasting results for the powers involved and the rising nations of the continent. Which one triumphs may have profound implications for all parties in the years ahead. The differences are, perhaps, nowhere as stark as in the world's newest nation, South Sudan.

A Midwife's Tale

Starting in the 1980s, the efforts of an eclectic, bipartisan collection of American supporters—Washington activists, evangelical Christians, influential congressional representatives, celebrities, a rising State Department star, a presidential administration focused on regime change and nation-building, and another that picked up the mantle—helped bring South Sudan into existence. *Midwife* was the word then-chair of the Senate Foreign Relations Committee John Kerry chose to describe the process.

In recent years, no country in Africa has received as much congressional attention. On July 9, 2011, South Sudan's Independence Day, President Barack Obama released a stirring statement. "I am confident that the bonds of friendship between South Sudan and the United States will only deepen in the years to come. As Southern Sudanese undertake the hard work of building their new country, the United States pledges our partnership as they seek the security, development, and responsive governance that can fulfill their aspirations and respect their human rights."

As the new nation broke away from Sudan after decades of bloody civil war, the United States poured in billions of dollars, including both humanitarian aid and military and security assistance. It also invested heavily in governmental institutions and built infrastructure (constructing or repairing roads and bridges). It sent military instructors to train the country's armed forces and advisors to mentor government officials. It helped beef up the education sector, worked to facilitate economic development and American investment, while opening the U.S. market to duty-free South Sudanese imports.

The new nation, it was hoped, would bolster US national security interests by injecting a heavy dose of democracy into the heart of Africa, while promoting political stability and good governance. Specifically, it was to serve as a democratic bulwark against Sudan and its president, Omar al-Bashir, who had once harbored Osama bin Laden and is wanted by the International Criminal Court for crimes against humanity in that country's Darfur region.

When South Sudan broke away, it took much of Sudan's oil wealth with it, becoming sub-Saharan Africa's third-largest oil producer behind Nigeria and Angola. In taking those resources out of Bashir's hands, it offered the promise of more energy stability in Africa. It was even expected to serve Washington's military aims—and soon, the United States began employing South Sudanese troops as proxies in a quest to destroy Joseph Kony's Lord's Resistance Army.

That was the dream, at least. But like Washington's regime change and nation-building projects in Iraq and Afghanistan, things soon started going very, very wrong. Today, South Sudan's armed forces are little more than a collection of competing militias that have fractured along ethnic lines and turned on each other. The country's political institutions and economy are in shambles, its oil production (which accounts for about 90 percent of government revenue) is crippled, corruption goes unchecked, towns have been looted and leveled during recent fighting, the nation is mired in a massive humanitarian crisis, famine looms, and interethnic relations may have been irreparably damaged.

The China Syndrome

During the years when America was helping bring South Sudan into existence, another world power also took an interest in the country—and a very different tack when it came to its development. After having invested a reported $20 billion in Sudan—a land long on the US sanctions blacklist—China watched as the new nation of South Sudan claimed about 75 percent of its oil fields. In 2012, newly inaugurated South Sudanese President Salva Kiir traveled to China, where he sipped champagne with then-President Hu Jintao and reportedly secured a pledge of $8 billion to build up his country's infrastructure and support its oil sector. (A top Chinese envoy later dismissed reports of such a sum, but hinted that China was willing to make even greater investments in the country if it achieved a lasting peace with its northern neighbor.)

Two years later, the China National Petroleum Corporation, with a 40 percent stake, is now the largest shareholder in the Greater Nile Petroleum Operating Company, the top oil consortium in South Sudan. It also leads another important consortium, the Greater Pioneer Operating Company. During the first ten months of 2013, China imported nearly 14 million barrels of oil from South Sudan. That adds up to about 77 percent of the country's crude oil output and twice as much as China imports from energy-rich Nigeria. While South Sudanese oil accounts for only about 5 percent of China's total petroleum imports, the country has nonetheless provided Beijing with a new African partner. This was especially useful as a US and NATO intervention in Libya in 2011 created chaotic conditions, causing China to suffer heavy losses ($20 billion according to Chinese sources) in various energy and other projects in that country.

"At the end of the day, China's main interest is stability so that they can function on a commercial basis. And to achieve that stability they've had to get more involved on the political side," says Cameron Hudson, director for African affairs on the staff of the National Security Council at the White House from 2005 to 2009. "They have a very large presence in Juba and are doing a lot of business beyond the oil sector."

In fact, just days before South Sudan plunged into civil war late in 2013, the deep-pocketed Export-Import Bank of China was reportedly preparing to offer the country $2 billion in loans and credit to build six key roads—including a 1,500-mile highway to link the capital, Juba, with Sudan's main port—crucial bridges across the Nile River, schools and hospitals in every county, a hydropower plant, a government conference center, and a staple of Chinese construction schemes in Africa, a stadium.

Recently, Chinese Premier Li Keqiang promised to expand cooperation with South Sudan in trade, agriculture, construction of infrastructure, and energy. Meanwhile, a separate $158 million deal to repair and expand the airport in Juba, financed by China's Export-Import Bank and carried out by a Chinese firm, was announced. In addition, China shipped nearly $40 million in arms—millions of rounds of ammunition, thousands of automatic rifles and grenade launchers, and hundreds of machine guns and pistols—to Salva Kiir's armed forces.

Continental Competition

China's interest in South Sudan is indicative of its relations with the continent as a whole. Beijing has long looked to Africa for diplomatic cooperation in the international arena and, with the continent accounting for more than 25 percent of the votes in the UN General Assembly, relied on it for political support. More recently, economics has become the paramount factor in the growing relationship between the rising Asian power and the continent.

Hungry for energy reserves, minerals, and other raw materials to fuel its domestic growth, China's Export-Import Bank and other state-controlled entities regularly offer financing for railroads, highways, and other major infrastructure projects, often tied to the use of Chinese companies and workers. In exchange, China expects long-term supplies of needed natural resources. Such relationships have exploded in the new century with its African trade jumping from $10 billion to an estimated $200 billion, far exceeding that of the United States or any European country. It has now been Africa's largest trading partner for the past five years and boasts of having struck $400 billion worth of deals in African construction projects which have already yielded almost 1,400 miles of railroad track and nearly 2,200 miles of highways.

Resources traded for infrastructure are, however, just one facet of China's expanding economic relationship with Africa. Looking down the road, Beijing increasingly sees the continent as a market for its manufacturing products. While the West ages and sinks deeper into debt, Africa is getting younger and growing at an exponential pace. Its population is, according to demographers, poised to double by the middle of the century, jumping to as many as 3.5 billion—larger than China and India combined—with working-age people far outnumbering the elderly and children.

With its ability to produce goods at low prices, China is betting on being a major supplier of a growing African market when it comes to food, clothes, appliances, and other consumer goods. As Howard French, author of *China's Second Continent*, notes, "a variety of economic indicators show that the fortunes of large numbers of Africans are improving dramatically and will likely continue to do so over the next decade or two, only faster." According to the International Monetary Fund, ten of the twenty economies projected to grow fastest from 2013 to 2017 are located in sub-Saharan Africa. In 2013, the World Bank attributed 60 percent of Africa's economic growth to consumer spending. Beijing may even fuel this rise further by relocating low-skilled, labor-intensive jobs to that continent as it develops more skilled manufacturing and high-tech industries at home.

One Chinese export integral to Beijing's dealings with Africa has, however, largely escaped notice. In the space of a decade, as French points out, one million or more Chinese have emigrated to Africa, buying up land, establishing businesses, plying just about every conceivable trade from medicine to farming to prostitution. These expats are altering the fundamentals of cultural and economic exchange across the continent and creating something wholly new. "For all of China's denials that its overseas ambitions could be compared to those of Europeans or Americans," writes French, "what I was witnessing in Africa is the higgledy-piggledy cobbling together of a new Chinese realm of interest. Here were the beginnings of a new empire."

This mass influx of Chinese pioneers has bred resentment in some quarters, as have heavy-handed tactics by Chinese compa-

nies that often ignore local labor laws and environmental regulations, freeze out local workers, mistreat them, or pay them exceptionally low wages. This, in turn, has led to instances of violence
against Africa's Chinese, as has Beijing's support for unpopular
and repressive governments. Such threats to the safety of Chinese
citizens and business interests, as well as general political instability and armed conflicts—from Libya to South Sudan—have given
China still another reason to build up its presence.

Traditionally, Beijing has adhered to a noninterference, "no
strings attached" foreign policy—meaning no requirements on
partner nations in terms of transparency, corruption, environmental protection, human rights, or good governance—and, as
opposed to the United States, has avoided overseas military in-
ventions. While it has long contributed to UN peacekeeping operations—the only kind of foreign intervention Beijing considers
legitimate—China has generally operated far from the front lines.
But things are subtly shifting on this score.

In 2011, after the US-backed revolution in Libya imperiled
30,000 Chinese living there, the People's Liberation Army coordinated air and sea assets in the largest evacuation mission in its
history. As the war in Libya destabilized neighboring Mali, China
sent combat troops—for the first time in its history—to join UN
forces in a bid to stabilize a nation that the United States had
spent a decade bolstering through counterterrorism funding.

Then, when US-backed South Sudan slid into civil war late last
year—and three hundred Chinese workers had to be evacuated—
Beijing departed from the hands-off approach it had taken only a
few years earlier with Sudan, ramped up diplomatic efforts, and
pushed hard for peace talks. "This is something new for us," said
China's special envoy to Africa, Zhong Jianhua. This was, he noted,
the beginning of a "new chapter" in policies by which China would

now "do more [in terms of] peace and security for this continent."

More recently, Beijing managed to broker an unprecedented arrangement to expand the mandate of the UN mission in South Sudan. In addition to "protection of civilians, monitoring and investigating human rights abuses, and facilitating the delivery of humanitarian assistance," according to *Foreign Policy*, "Beijing quietly secured a deal that will put the U.N.'s famed blue helmets to work protecting workers in South Sudan's oil installations, where China has invested billions of dollars." Although protecting the oil fields is akin to taking the government's side in a civil war, the United States, France, and Great Britain backed the plan to protect oil installations under a UN mandate, citing the importance of the energy sector to the future of the country. In return, China will send an 850-man infantry battalion to bolster the UN mission, adding to the 350 military personnel it already had on the ground here.

When it comes to protecting their infrastructure, "the Chinese have gotten very good at deploying peacekeeping forces," Patricia Taft, a senior associate with the Fund for Peace, tells TomDispatch. "The Chinese have, in East Africa and also West Africa, inserted themselves as a security presence, mainly to protect their oil interests, their infrastructure, or whatever economic projects they're deeply invested in."

Yun Sun, a fellow at the Stimson Center and an expert on China's relations with Africa, doesn't see these recent developments as a militarization of China's mission but as a symptom of increased investment in the countries of the continent. "China cares more about security issues in Africa . . . due to its own national interests," Sun says. "It means China will contribute more to the peace and security issues of the continent." And it seems that Beijing is now doing so, in part on America's dime.

Winners and Losers

US taxpayers, who fund about 27 percent of the cost of UN peacekeeping missions, are now effectively underwriting China's efforts to protect its oil interests in South Sudan. Washington continues to pour aid into that country—more than $456 million in humanitarian assistance in fiscal year 2014—while China has pledged far less in humanitarian relief. Meanwhile, Juba has tied itself ever more tightly to Chinese energy interests, with plans to borrow more than $1 billion from oil companies to keep the government afloat as it battles the rebels.

Taft sees these deals with largely Chinese firms as risky for South Sudan's future and potentially ineffective as well. "It's putting a band-aid on a hemorrhaging artery," she says. David Deng, research director for the South Sudan Law Society, echoes this: "We're mortgaging our children's future to fight a pointless war."

South Sudan seems emblematic of a larger trend in the race between Washington and Beijing in Africa. In 2000, China's trade there passed $10 billion for the first time and has been growing at a 30 percent clip annually ever since. Nine years later, China overtook the United States to become the continent's largest trading partner and, by 2012, its trade was nearly double that of the United States—$198.5 billion to $99.8 billion.

For the Chinese, Africa is El Dorado, a land of opportunity for one million migrants. For America, it's a collection of "ungoverned spaces," "austere locations," and failing states increasingly dominated by local terror groups poised to become global threats, a danger zone to be militarily managed through special operators and proxy armies. "In Africa, terrorists, criminal organizations, militias, corrupt officials, and pirates continue to exploit ungoverned and under-governed territory on the continent and its surrounding waters," reads the Pentagon's 2014 Quadrennial Defense Review (QDR). "The potential for rapidly developing threats, particularly in fragile states, including violent public protests and terrorist attacks, could pose acute challenges to U.S. interests."

"Recent engagements in Somalia and Mali, in which African countries and regional organizations are working together with international partners in Europe and the United States, may provide a model for future partnerships," adds the QDR. But a look at those poster-child nations for US involvement—one in East and one in West Africa—instead provides evidence of America's failings on the continent.

In 2006, the Islamic Court Union (ICU), a loose confederation of indigenous Islamist groups seeking to impose order on the failed state of Somalia, defeated the Alliance for Restoration of Peace and Counterterrorism, a US-supported militia, and pushed US-backed warlords out of Mogadishu, the capital. In response, the United States green-lighted a 2007 invasion of the country by Ethiopia's military and secretly sent in a small contingent of its own troops (still operating in Somalia to this day). This succeeded only in splintering the ICU, sending its moderates into exile, while its hardliners formed a far more extreme Islamic group, al-Shabab, which became the key Muslim resistance force against Washington's Ethiopian proxies.

Al-Shabab experienced a great deal of military success before being beaten back by the Ethiopians, troops from a US-supported Somali transitional government, and well-armed peacekeepers from the US-backed African Union mission in Somalia (AMISOM). These forces were, from 2009 onward, joined by proxies trained and armed by US ally Kenya, whose own army invaded the country in 2011. Their forces in Somalia, eventually folded into the AMISOM mission, are still deployed there. On the run and outgunned, al-Shabab responded by threatening to take the war beyond its borders and soon began to do so.

In other words, what started as a local Islamic group achieving, according to a Chatham House report, "the unthinkable, uniting Mogadishu for the first time in 16 years, and reestablishing peace and security," quickly became a transnational terror organization in the wake of the Ethiopian invasion and other acts of intervention. In 2010, al-Shabab carried out a bomb attack in Uganda as a punishment for that country's contribution to AMISOM. In 2011, it launched an escalating series of shootings, grenade attacks, and bombings in Kenya. The next year, the formerly Somalia-centric outfit further internationalized its efforts as one of its leaders pledged obedience to al-Qaeda chief Ayman al-Zawahiri. In 2013, the group carried out a devastating attack on the Westgate Mall in Kenya that killed sixty-seven.

In May 2014, al-Shabab extended its reach even further with its first-ever suicide attack in Djibouti, the tiny Horn of Africa nation that contributes troops to AMISOM and hosts French troops, a key European proxy force for Washington on the continent. "The attack was carried out against the French Crusaders for their complicity in the massacres and persecution of our Muslim brothers in the Central African Republic and for their active role in training and equipping the apostate Djiboutian troops in Somalia," read an al-Shabab statement that also highlighted a US-backed French military mission in the Central African Republic.

In the months since, the group repeatedly launched murderous assaults on civilians in Kenya and continues to threaten Uganda and Burundi, which also contributes troops to AMISOM, with future attacks. It has even gained regional affiliates, like Al-Hijra, an underground group accused of recruiting for al-Shabab in Kenya.

After 9/11, on the opposite side of the continent, US programs like the Pan-Sahel Initiative and the Trans-Saharan Counterterrorism Partnership pumped hundreds of millions of dollars into training and arming the militaries of Mali, Niger, Chad, Mauritania, Nigeria, Algeria, and Tunisia, again in order to promote regional "stability." While US Special Operations forces were teaching infantry tactics to Malian troops, the Chinese were engaging very differently with that West African nation. Despite Mali's lack of natural resources, China constructed a key bridge, a hospital, a stadium, a major government building, several factories, miles of highways, and a $230 million waterworks project.

The United States wasn't, however, left totally out in the cold on the construction front. The State Department's Millennium Challenge Corporation (MCC), for example, spent $71.6 million to expand the Bamako Airport. The contract, however, went to a Chinese firm—as did many MCC contracts across Africa—because American companies were uninterested in working there despite guaranteed US financing.

What Washington was trying to build in Mali came crashing down, however, after its Libyan intervention. Nomadic Tuareg fighters looted the weapons stores of the Gaddafi regime they had previously served, crossed the border, routed US-backed Malian forces, and seized the northern part of the country. This, in turn, prompted a US-trained officer to stage a military coup in the Malian capital, Bamako, and oust the democratically elected president.

Soon after, the Tuareg rebels were muscled aside by heavily armed Islamist rebels who began taking over the country. This prompted the United States to back a 2013 invasion by French and African forces which arrested the complete collapse of Mali—leaving it in a permanent state of occupation and low-level insurgency. Meanwhile, Islamist fighters and Gaddafi's weapons were scattered across Africa, contributing to greater instability in Nigeria and Libya, as well as increased threat levels in Chad, Burkina Faso, Ghana, Guinea, Niger, Senegal, and Togo. It evidently also spurred an audacious revenge attack in Algeria that left more than eighty dead and an assault on a French-run uranium mine and a nearby military base in Niger in which at least twenty-five people were killed.

Two Systems, One Continent

For all the time spent training proxies, all the propaganda efforts, all the black ops missions, all the counterterror funds, the results have been dismal for the United States. A glance at the official State Department list of terrorist organizations indicates that these efforts have been mirrored by the growth of radical militant groups, including the Libyan Islamic Fighting Group added in 2004; al-Shabab in 2008; Ansar al-Dine, Boko Haram, Ansaru, and the al-Mulathamun Battalion in 2013; and Libya's Ansar al-Shari'a in Benghazi, Ansar al-Shari'a in Darnah, Ansar al-Shari'a in Tunisia, and the Egyptian militant group Ansar Bayt al-Maqdis, all in 2014. And that's hardly a full list. Not included are various terror organizations, rebel forces, separatist movements, armed groups, and militias like the Movement for Unity and Jihad in West Africa, fighters from the group formerly known as Seleka and their rivals, anti-balaka militiamen in the Central African Republic, Taureg separatists of Mali's National Movement for the Liberation of Azawad, the Congolese Resistance Patriots, Burundi's National Forces of Liberation, and others.

Over these years, as the United States has chased terror groups and watched them proliferate, China has taken another route, devoting its efforts to building goodwill through public works and winning over governments through "no strings attached" policies.

"Our goal is not to counter China; our goal is not to contain China," President Obama said during a trip to Asia earlier this year. In South Sudan, as in Africa as a whole, Washington seems increasingly unable to even keep up. "On certain levels, we can't or won't compete with China," says the Fund for Peace's Patricia Taft. "China will continue to eclipse us in terms of economic interests in Africa." The United States is, however, still preeminent in the political sphere and that influence, she says, will continue to trump anything China can currently offer.

The question is: For how long?

Cameron Hudson, formerly of the National Security Council and now the acting director of the Center for the Prevention of Genocide at the US Holocaust Museum, thinks strengthening partnerships with the Chinese could lead to major dividends for the United States. "They have more skin in the game," he says of Beijing's relationship with South Sudan. "They have a growing set of interests there."

Benediste Hoareau, head of political affairs for the East African Standby Force—a rapid intervention force in-the-making, consisting of troops from the region's militaries—expresses similar sentiments. He believes in the often repeated axiom of finding African solutions to African problems and says that foreign powers should provide the funds and let African forces do the fighting and peacekeeping in South Sudan.

Hoareau, in fact, sees no need for a new cold war or any other kind of contest between the foreign titans here. There are plenty of opportunities for both the United States and China in Africa and in South Sudan, he tells TomDispatch. A rivalry between the two powers can only bring trouble. "They're elephants," Hoareau says of China and America, "and you know just who will get trampled."

10

Christmas in July and the Collapse of America's Great African Experiment: As a Man-Made Famine Looms, Christmas Comes Early to South Sudan

August 7, 2014

Juba, South Sudan. The soft glow of the dancing white lights is a dead giveaway. It's Christmas in July at the US Embassy compound. Behind high walls topped with fierce-looking metal impediments meant to discourage climbers, there's a party under way.

Close your eyes and you could be at a Stateside summer barbecue or an office holiday party. Even with them open, the local realities of dirt roads and dirty water, civil war, mass graves, and nightly shoot-to-kill curfews seem foreign. These walls, it turns out, are even higher than they look.

Out by the swimming pool and the well-stocked bar, every table is packed with people. Slightly bleary-eyed men and sun-kissed women wear Santa hats and decorations in their hair. One festive fellow is dressed as Cousin Eddie from *National Lampoon's Christmas Vacation* complete with a white sweater, black dickey, and bright white loafers. Another is straddling an inflatable killer whale that he's borrowed from the collection of playthings around the pool. He's using it as an improvised chair while he stuffs his face from an all-American smorgasbord. We're all eating well tonight. Mac and cheese, barbecued ribs, beef tenderloin, fried chicken, mashed potatoes and gravy, green beans, and for dessert, peach cobbler. The drinks are flowing, too: wine and whisky and fine Tusker beer.

Yuletide songs drift out into the sultry night in this, the capital of the world's newest nation. "Simply having a wonderful Christmastime," croons Paul McCartney.

Just minutes away, near the airport in an area known as Tongping, things aren't quite so wonderful. There's no fried chicken, no ribs, no peach cobbler. At Juba's UN camp for internally displaced persons (IDPs), they're eating sorghum and a crude porridge made from a powdered blend of corn and soybeans provided by the UN World Food Program. Children at the camp call it "the yellow food." "It's no good," one of them tells me, with a quick head shake for emphasis.

I mention to a few of the embassy revelers that I'm heading several hundred miles north to Malakal. A couple of them assure me that, according to colleagues, it's "not that bad." But while we're chowing down, an emaciated young girl in Malakal clings to life. This one-year-old arrived at the hospital run by Médecins Sans Frontières (Doctors Without Borders, or MSF) at the

UN camp there several days earlier, severely malnourished and weighing just eleven pounds. It's uncertain if she'll survive. One in ten children who arrive at the hospital in her condition don't.

A Man-Made Famine

As John Kerry, then chair of the Senate Foreign Relations Committee, put it in 2012, the United States "helped midwife the birth" of South Sudan. The choice of words may have been cringe-worthy, but hardly divorced from reality. For more than twenty years, a bipartisan coalition in Washington and beyond championed rebel forces here.

It would be Washington's major nation-building effort in Africa, a new country destined to join Iraq and Afghanistan as a regional bulwark of democracy and a shining example of American know-how. On South Sudan's independence day, July 9, 2011, President Obama hailed the moment as a "time of hope" and pledged US partnership to the new land, emphasizing security and development. There's precious little evidence of either of these at the UN camps and even less in vast areas of the countryside now teetering on the edge of a catastrophic famine.

Since a civil war broke out in December 2013, at least 10,000 South Sudanese have been killed, untold numbers of women and girls have been victims of sexual violence, and atrocities have been committed by all parties to the conflict. As a result, in the eyes of the United Nations, in a world of roiling strife—civil wars, mass killings, hunger, and conflicts from Iraq to Gaza, Ukraine to Libya—South Sudan is, along with the Central African Republic and Syria, one of just three "L3 emergencies," the world's most severe, large-scale humanitarian crises. The country has also just displaced Somalia—for six years running the archetypal failed state—atop the Fund for Peace's 178-nation list of the world's most fragile nations.

Today, close to 100,000 people are huddled on UN military bases around the country, just a fraction of the almost 1.5 million who have been put to flight and are waiting out the war as internal exiles or as refugees in the bordering nations of Uganda, Ethiopia, Kenya, and Sudan. Such massive levels of displacement guarantee another nightmare to come. Since so many subsistence farmers weren't around to plant their crops, despite fertile ground and sufficient rain, seeds never met soil and food never had a chance to grow.

"At this point in time, because it's the rainy season, there's nothing we can do in terms of agriculture," says Caroline Saint-Mleux, the regional emergency coordinator for East and Central Africa at CARE International. Above us, the sky is darkening as we sit in plastic chairs in the muddy "humanitarian hub," a grimy ghetto of white tents, nondescript trailers, and makeshift headquarters of aid agencies like the International Committee of the Red Cross and MSF, on the outer edge of the UN base at Malakal. Her organization did distribute a limited number of seeds to farmers still on their land earlier in the year, but can do no more. The planting season is long past. "It would be a waste of energy at this point," she says, resignation in her voice.

Famine "is a very realistic possibility," Deborah Schein tells me. She's the coordinator for the United Nations in Upper Nile State, where Malakal is located. Right now, experts are crunching the numbers and debating whether to formally declare a famine. Whether it's done in the fall of 2014 or sometime in 2015, aid workers say, it's definitely coming and the sooner it comes, the more lives can be saved. Recently, UN Security Council president Eugène-Richard Gasana called attention to "the catastrophic food

Women walk through the muddy UN mission in South Sudan camp in Malakal. (Nick Turse)

insecurity situation." Already 3.9 million people—about one in three South Sudanese—face dangerous levels of food insecurity. However, unlike in Ethiopia in the 1980s, where drought led to crop failures that killed a million people, Vanessa Parra, Oxfam America's press liaison in South Sudan, says this country is facing an "entirely man-made famine."

Nyajuma's Story

If it were dry, it would take only five minutes to walk from Deborah Schein's office at the UN base in Malakal to the Médecins Sans Frontières field hospital in the adjoining IDP camp where 17,000 South Sudanese are now taking refuge. But the rains have turned this ground into fetid mud and an easy walk into a slip-sliding slog.

At the end of a gray, mucky expanse that nearly sucks the boots off your feet, an MSF flag flies outside a barn-sized white tent. Before you enter, you need to visit a foot-washing station, then have your feet or boots disinfected. Even then, it's impossible to keep the grime out. "As you can imagine, this is not the best environment for a hospital," says Teresa Sancristoval, the energetic chief of MSF's emergency operations in Malakal.

Step inside that tent and you're immediately in a ward that's electric with activity. It's hard to believe that this twenty-four-hour-a-day, seven-day-a-week hospital is manned by only three expat doctors and three expat nurses, plus a medical team leader. Still, add in various support personnel, local staff, and the many patients and suddenly this giant tent begins to shrink, putting space at a premium.

"The great majority of the hospital is pediatrics," says Sancristoval, a compact dynamo from Madrid with the bearing of a field general and intense eyes. Not that she even needs to point that out. In this first ward, the fifteen metal-frame beds—blue paint peeling, thin mattresses, four makeshift bamboo posts topped with mosquito nets—are packed tight, all but two filled with mother and child or children. Some days, there's not a bed to spare, leaving patients ill with infection and wracked by disease to sleep on whatever space can be found on the floor.

On a bed adjacent to the main thoroughfare sits a tiny girl in a yellow top and pink skirt, her head bandaged and covered in a clingy mesh net. Nyajuma has been in this hospital for two weeks. She was lying here inside this tent, wasted and withered, the night we were having our Christmas feast at the embassy about 400 miles south in Juba.

Nyajuma weighed only eleven pounds on arrival. According to the American Academy of Pediatrics, the average one-year-old girl in the United States. weighs more than double that. She was quickly started on the first of two powdered therapeutic foods to combat her severe malnutrition, followed by a regimen of Plumpy'Nut, a high-protein, high-calorie peanut paste, four times a day along with two servings of milk.

It would have been bad enough if her only problem were severe malnutrition, but that condition also exacerbated the skin infection beneath the bandages on her head. In addition, she suffers from kala azar, a deadly disease caused by a parasite spread by sandflies that results in prolonged fever and weakness. On top of that, she is being treated for two other potentially lethal maladies, cholera and tuberculosis. Her mother, resting beside her, looks exhausted, world-beaten. Pregnant on arrival, she gave birth five days later. She lies next to Nyajuma, listless, but carefully covers her face with her arm as if to shield herself from the harsh world beyond this bed.

During her first week at the hospital, nurse Monica Alvarez tells me, Nyajuma didn't crack a smile. "But now, voilà," she says lifting the child, sparking a broad grin that reflects the sea change in her condition. Nyajuma is enduring the rigors of kala azar and tuberculosis treatments with great aplomb. "She's eating well and she's smiling all the time," says Alvarez, who's quick with a smile herself. But Nyajuma is still in the early stages of treatment. Once stable, severely malnourished children can be transferred to ambulatory care. But it takes roughly six weeks for them to make a full recovery and be discharged. And in today's South Sudan, they are the lucky ones.

Of those who make it to the hospital in such a condition, 10 percent don't survive, Javier Roldan, MSF's medical team leader, tells me. "We have people who come in in later stages or have a co-infection because malnutrition has compromised their immune system, which makes treatment much more complicated." He talks of the difficulty of losing patients for want of better facilities, more staff, and greater resources. "The outcome of a baby

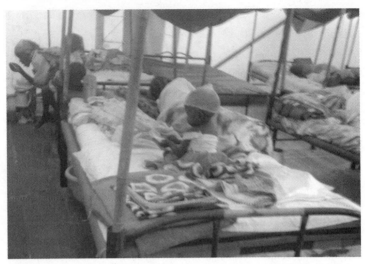

One-year-old Nyajuma sits on a bed next to her mother at the Médecins Sans Frontières hospital at the UN mission in South Sudan camp in Malakal.

weighing one and a half kilos [3.3 pounds] in Europe or America would be no problem at all, but here there's quite a high mortality rate," says Roldan. "It's very frustrating for the medical staff when you have patients die because you don't have the means to treat them."

Malakal is no anomaly. At the MSF feeding station in Leer, a town in adjoining Unity State, they've treated roughly 1,800 malnourished children since mid-May, compared to 2,300 in all of last year. North of Leer, in Bentiu, the site of repeated spasms of violence, the situation is especially grim. "Over five percent of the children are suffering from severe acute malnutrition," says CARE's Country Director for South Sudan Aimee Ansari. "On the day I left Bentiu, CARE helped parents transport the bodies of children who had died from malnutrition to a burial site." In all, according to the UN Children's Fund (UNICEF) and the UN World Food Program (WFP), almost one million South Sudanese children under five years of age will require treatment for acute malnutrition in 2014. UNICEF projects that 50,000 of them could die.

The Camps and the Countryside

At the UN's Tongping camp in Juba—where nearly 11,500 of the area's tens of thousands of internally displaced persons are taking refuge—the food situation is "not very good at all." So John, a seventeen-year-old resident, emphatically assures me beneath the relentless midday sun. "Outside, when I was living at home, we could have fruit or whatever we wanted." Here, he eats no fresh food and no vegetables. Its sorghum and "the yellow food" mixed with sugar, oil, and water. "This food doesn't even compare," he says more than once.

Still, people here aren't dying of malnutrition and even those in the ruder, more dismal camps in Bentiu and Malakal are luckier than most since they have access to aid from NGOs. At a time when South Sudan needs them most, however, almost eight months of war, insecurity, and attacks on aid workers have severely limited the reach of humanitarian organizations. Speaking of the entire NGO community, Wendy Taeuber, country director for the International Rescue Committee in South Sudan, says, "The remoteness of rural areas of South Sudan combined with the rainy season means that there are hundreds of thousands of IDPs still in need of additional assistance."

Sitting in the trailer that serves as his office, I ask Paulin Nkwosseu, the chief field officer for UNICEF in Malakal, about the situation of those in less accessible areas along the Nile River where WFP distributions are limited. "Due to the crisis, people have no income and no food, so they're surviving on monthly food distributions from WFP," he tells me. "But they say that the food distributed by WFP is not sufficient for the whole family."

UNICEF works with NGO partners to reach people outside the camps, but it's a struggle. Nkwosseu walks over to a large wall map and begins to point out Nile River towns to the north like Wau Shilluk (currently suffering a cholera outbreak), Lul, Kodok, and Melut. These, he says, are hubs where South Sudanese from rural areas go when faced with hunger. The reason is simple enough: the river is one of the few viable transport options in a country the size of Texas that has almost no paved roads and whose dirt tracks in the rainy season are quickly reduced to impassable mud.

Even using the Nile is anything but a slam-dunk operation. Earlier this year, for instance, a convoy of barges transporting food and fuel to Malakal was attacked by armed men. Absent the acts of rebels, soldiers, or bandits, food barges are still regularly delayed by everything from mechanical issues to drawn-out negotiations with local powerbrokers. Air drops are costly, impractical, and—thanks to a lack of airfield infrastructure—often unfeasible. Security is minimal and so thousands of tons of food stocks have simply been looted. Even when road transport is possible, vehicles are attacked and food is stolen by both government and rebel troops, eager to feed themselves. When food supplies do make it to the river towns, many in need are unlikely to make it in from the water-logged countryside in time.

America's Limits

Among African nations, South Sudan has had an almost unprecedented relationship with the United States. Aside from Liberia—a nation settled, hundreds of years ago, by former American slaves, whose capital Monrovia is named after a US president—it is the only African country for which Americans have evidenced a deep bipartisan commitment and "long-standing humanitarian and political interest as well as a deeper kinship," says Cameron Hudson.

"For nearly a decade leading up to the 2011 declaration of independence, the cause of the nation and its citizens was one that was near and dear to the heart of two successive U.S. administrations and some of its most seasoned and effective thinkers and policymakers," Patricia Taft, a senior associate with the Fund for Peace, wrote in a recent analysis of South Sudan. "In order to secure this nation-building 'win,' both the George W. Bush and Obama administrations poured tons of aid into South Sudan, in every form imaginable. From military aid to food aid to the provision of technical expertise, America was South Sudan's biggest ally and backer, ardently midwifing the country into nationhood by whatever means necessary."

For all America's efforts, the wheels started coming off almost immediately. "We've gotten pretty good at understanding what goes into building a state, institutionally, but as far as what creates a nation that's actually functional, we fell short," Taft tells TomDispatch. The United States, she says, failed to do the necessary heavy lifting to encourage the building of a shared national identity and sat on its hands when targeted interventions might have helped reverse worrisome developments in South Sudan.

Still, the United States repeatedly pledged unyielding support for the struggling young nation. In August 2012, for example, Secretary of State Hillary Clinton, speaking in Juba, was emphatic that the US "commitment to this new nation is enduring and absolute in terms of assistance and aid and support going forward." A year later, announcing the appointment of Donald Booth as President Obama's Special Envoy for Sudan and South

Sudan, Clinton's successor, John Kerry, made special reference to America's "enduring commitment" to the South Sudanese people.

Lately, however, phrases like "enduring and absolute" have been replaced by the language of limits. Speaking in Juba just days before the July Christmas party, US Assistant Secretary of State for Population, Refugees, and Migration Anne Richard drew attention to the fact that the United States had given generously to South Sudan, but that such assistance would be of little use if the war continues. "There is a limit to how much aid can be provided in a year with so many crises around the world," she said.

That doesn't bode well for those already going hungry and those who will be affected by the coming famine. Here, limits equal lives lost. A $1.8 billion UN aid operation designed to counter the immediate, life-threatening needs of the worst affected South Sudanese is currently just 50 percent funded, according to Amanda Weyler of the UN Office for the Coordination of Humanitarian Affairs in South Sudan. She explains that "any shortfall in funding potentially means that we cannot save lives of people that we may otherwise have been able to help."

In a statement emailed to TomDispatch, Anne Richard acknowledged this very point, though she couched it in the language of "needs," not lives. She put the blame on South Sudan's warring factions while lamenting the plethora of crises around the world. "Even if Congress again funds our budget so that we can provide a solid share of support to aid organizations and U.N. appeals, we can't cover them completely and other donor countries will also be stretched. At some point, we may see reports of food and water shortages and healthcare needs going unaddressed," she wrote. "Ultimately, these crises are man-made and will not be alleviated until the fighting stops."

Do They Know It's Christmastime at All?

It's an overcast day, but the sun is strong behind the clouds and it's bright inside the white tent of the Médecins Sans Frontières field hospital. It's also hot. One of several large, aged metal fans pushes the heavy, humid air around these cramped quarters as the staff moves purposefully from patient to patient, checking progress, dispensing medicine, providing instructions. Children cry and shriek, babble and laugh, and cough and cough and cough.

A scrawny black and white cat slips through a maze of legs, moving from the rudimentary pharmacy to the examination room past the bed where Nyajuma sits. She's putting on weight, two and a half pounds since her arrival and so, for her, things are looking somewhat better. But as the country plunges into famine, how many other Nyajumas will arrive here and find there's not enough food, not enough medicine, too few doctors? How many others will never make it and simply die in the bush?

"When there's a clash, when the conflict starts, it's in the news every day. Then we start to forget about it. In South Sudan, the needs are only getting bigger, even bigger than in the beginning," MSF's Javier Roldan tells me. "When the conflict becomes chronic, the situation deteriorates. Food access is getting even more difficult. Fewer donors are providing money, so the situation for civilians is deteriorating day by day."

That embassy party in Juba seems light-years away, not just in another state but another world—a world where things in Malakal don't seem so bad. It's a world where choice cuts of beef sizzle and cold lager flows and the pool looks cool and inviting, a world where limits on aid are hard realities to be dispassionately explained and cursorily lamented, not death sentences to be suffered.

From Iraq to Afghanistan, American-style nation-building has crumbled, exposing the limits of American power. Before things are over in South Sudan, Washington's great experiment in Africa may prove to be the most disastrous effort of all. Just three years after this country's independence, two years after Hillary Clinton stood in this city and pledged enduring and absolute assistance, at a time when its people are most in need, the United States is talking about limits on aid, about backing away from the country it fostered, its prime example of nation-building-in-action in the heart of Africa. The effects will be felt from Juba to Jonglei, Bor to Bentiu, Malek to Malakal.

If things continue as they have, by the time the US Embassy throws its actual Christmas bash, the civil war in South Sudan will have entered its second year and large swaths of the country might be months into a man-made famine abetted by an under-funded humanitarian response—and it's the most vulnerable, like Nyajuma, who will bear the brunt of the crisis. Experts are currently debating if—or when—famine can be declared. Doing so will exert additional pressure on funders and no doubt save lives, so a declaration can't come fast enough for Kate Donovan of UNICEF in South Sudan. "Waiting for data to be crunched in order to make sure all the numbers add up to famine is deadly for small children," she says. "It is like ringing fire alarms when the building is already burnt to the ground."

If history is any guide and projections of 50,000 child malnutrition fatalities are accurate, the outlook for South Sudan is devastating. What Donovan tells me should make Washington—and the rest of the world—sit up and take notice: "Half the kids may already be dead by the time famine is actually declared."

11

American Monuments
to Failure in Africa?
How Not to Win Hearts and Minds

September 7, 2014

DAR ES SALAAM, Tanzania. Movie night in Mouloud, Djibouti. Skype lessons in Ethiopia. Veterinary training assistance in Garissa, Kenya. And in this country on the east coast of Africa, work on both primary and secondary schools and a cistern to provide clean water. These are all-American good works, but who is doing them—and why?

As I sit in a room filled with scores of high-ranking military officers resplendent in their dress uniforms—Kenyans in their khakis, Burundians and Ugandans clad in olive, Tanzanians in deep forest green sporting like-colored berets and red epaulets with crossed rifles on their shoulders—chances are that the US military is carrying out some mission somewhere on this vast continent. It might be a kidnapping raid or a training exercise. It could be an airstrike or the construction of a drone base. Or, as I wait for the next speaker to approach the lectern at the Land Forces East Africa conference in Dar es Salaam, it could be a humanitarian operation run not by civilians in the aid business but by military troops with ulterior motives—part of a near-continent-wide campaign using the core tenets of counterinsurgency strategy.

The United States is trying to win a war for the hearts and minds of Africa. But a Pentagon investigation suggests that those mystery projects somewhere out there in Djibouti or Ethiopia or Kenya or here in Tanzania may well be orphaned, ill-planned, and undocumented failures in the making. According to the Department of Defense's watchdog agency, US military officials in Africa "did not adequately plan or execute" missions designed to win over Africans deemed vulnerable to the lures of violent extremism.

This evidence of failure in the earliest stages of the US military's hearts-and-minds campaign should have an eerie resonance for anyone who has followed its previous efforts to use humanitarian aid and infrastructure projects to sway local populations in Vietnam, Iraq, or Afghanistan. In each case, the operations failed in spectacular ways, but were only fully acknowledged after years of futility and billions of dollars in waste. In Africa, a war zone about which most Americans are completely unaware, the writing is already on the wall. Or at least it should be. While Pentagon investigators identified a plethora of problems, their report has, in fact, been kept under wraps for almost a year, while the command responsible for the failures has ignored all questions about it from TomDispatch.

Doing a Bad Job at Good Works

Today, as the US military increasingly confronts Africa as a "bat-tlefield," a significant number of its operations there have taken on the form of a textbook hearts-and-minds campaign that harkens back to failed US efforts in Southeast Asia during the 1960s and 1970s and more recently in the greater Middle East. In Vietnam, the so-called civilian half of the war—building schools, handing out soap, and offering rudimentary medical care—was obliter-ated by American heavy firepower that wiped out homes, whole hamlets, and whatever goodwill had been gained. As a result, U.S. counterinsurgency doctrine was tossed into the military's dust-bin—only to be resurrected decades later, as the Iraq War raged, by then-general and later CIA Director David Petraeus.

In 2005–2006, Petraeus oversaw the revision of FM 3-24, the military's counterinsurgency (COIN) field manual, and a resulting revolution in military affairs. Soon, American military officers in Iraq and Afghanistan were throwing large sums of money at com-plex problems, once again with the objective of winning hearts and minds. They bought off Sunni insurgents and poured billions of dollars into nation-building efforts, ranging from a modern chicken processing plant to a fun-in-the-sun water park, trying to refashion the rubble of a failed state into a functioning one.

As with Petraeus's career, which imploded amid scandal, the efforts he fostered similarly went down in flames. In Iraq, the chicken processing plant proved to be a Potemkin operation and the much ballyhooed Baghdad water park quickly fell into ruin. The country soon followed. Three years after the US withdrawal, Iraq teeters on the brink of catastrophe as most of Petraeus's Sun-ni mercenaries stood aside while the brutal Islamic State carved a portion of its caliphate from the country, and others, aggrieved with the US-backed government in Baghdad, sided with them. In Afghanistan, the results have been similarly dismal as America's hearts-and-minds monies yielded roads to nowhere (when they haven't already deteriorated into "death traps"); crumbling buildings; over crowded, underfunded, and teacher-less schools; and billions poured down the drain in one boondoggle after another.

In Africa, the sums and scale are far smaller, but the efforts are from the same counterinsurgency playbook. In fact, to the US military, humanitarian assistance—from medical care to infrastructure projects—is a form of "security cooperation." According to the latest edition of FM 3-24, published earlier this year:

> When these activities are used to defeat an insurgency, they are part of a counterinsurgency operation. While not all security cooperation activities are in support of counterinsurgency, security cooperation can be an effective counterinsurgency tool. These activities help the U.S. and the host nation gain credibility and help the host nation build legitimacy. These efforts can help prevent insurgencies.

AFRICOM and its subordinate command, Combined Joint Task Force–Horn of Africa (CJTF-HOA) based at Camp Lemonnier in Djibouti, have spent years engaged in such COIN-style humanitarian projects. Take a cursory glance at AFRICOM's official news releases and you'll find them crammed with feel-good stories like an effort by CJTF-HOA personnel to tutor would-be Djiboutian hotel workers in English or a joint effort by the State Department, AFRICOM, and the Army Corps of Engineers to build six new schools in Togo. Such acts are never framed in the context of counterinsurgency nor with an explicit link to US efforts to win hearts and minds. And never is there any mention of failings or fiascos.

However, an investigation by the Department of Defense's inspector general, completed in October 2013 but never publicly released, found failures in planning, executing, tracking, and documenting such projects. The restricted report, obtained by TomDispatch, describes a flawed system plagued by a variety of deeply embedded problems.

In some cases, military officials failed to identify how their projects even supported AFRICOM's objectives on the continent; in others, financial documentation was missing; in still others, CJTF-HOA personnel failed to ensure that local populations were equipped to keep the small-scale projects running or effective once the Americans moved on. The risk, the report suggests, is that these signs of Washington's goodwill and good intentions will quickly fall into disrepair and become what one American official called "monuments to US failure" in Africa.

AFRICOM reacted defensively. In an internal memo, Colonel Bruce Nickle, the acting chief of staff of US Africa Command, criticized the inspector general's methodology, questioned the inspector general's expertise, and suggested that some of the findings were "misleading." Close to a year after the report's release, neither AFRICOM nor CJTF-HOA has announced policy changes based on its recommendations. Repeated requests, over a period of months, by TomDispatch to AFRICOM media chief Benjamin Benson and the CJTF-HOA Public Affairs office for comment, further information, or clarification about the report as well as a request to interview Nickle have all gone unanswered.

COIN and the Fountains

Across Africa, the US military has engaged in a panoply of aid projects with an eye toward winning a war of ideas in the minds of Africans and so beating back the lure of extremist ideologies. These so-called civil-military operations (CMOs) include "humanitarian assistance" projects like the construction or repair of schools, water wells, and waste treatment systems, and "humanitarian and civic assistance" (HCA) efforts, like offering dental and veterinary care.

Kindness may be its own reward, but in the case of the US military, CMO benevolence is designed to influence foreign governments and civilian populations in order to "facilitate military operations and achieve U.S. objectives." According to the Pentagon, humanitarian assistance efforts are engineered to improve "U.S. visibility, access, and influence with foreign military and civilian counterparts," while HCA projects are designed to "promote the security and foreign policy interests of the United States." In the bureaucratic world of the US military, these small-scale efforts are further divided into "community relations activities," like the distribution of sports equipment, and "low-cost activities" such as seminars on solar panel maintenance or English-language discussion groups. Theoretically at least, add all these projects together and you've taken a major step toward winning Africans away from the influence of extremists. But are these projects working at all? Has anyone even bothered to check?

In a report titled "Combined Joint Task Force-Horn of Africa Needed Better Guidance and Systems to Adequately Manage Civil-Military Operations," the Department of Defense's inspector general found record keeping by the US military in Africa so abysmal that its officials "did not have an effective system to manage or report community relations and low cost activities." A spreadsheet supposedly tracking community low-cost activities during 2012 and 2013 was so incomplete that 43 percent of such efforts went unmentioned.

Nonetheless, the inspector general did manage to review 49 of 137 identified humanitarian assistance and civic assistance projects, which cost US taxpayers about $9 million, and found that the military officials overseeing CMO "did not adequately plan or execute" them in accordance with AFRICOM's "objectives." Close to 20 percent of the time, CJTF-HOA even failed to accurately explain the possible relationship of specific projects to objectives like countering extremist organizations or expanding AFRICOM's "network of partners on the continent." Examining sixty-six community relations and low-cost activities, investigators found that CJTF-HOA had failed to accurately identify their strategic objectives for, or maintained limited documentation on, 62 percent of them.

The task force also failed to report or could not provide information on expenditures for four of six projects selected for special review, despite a requirement to do so and the use of a computerized system specifically designed to track such information. These projects—two schools and a clinic in Djibouti as well as a school in Ethiopia—cost American taxpayers almost $1.3 million, yet US officials failed to properly account for where all that money actually went. All told, officials were unable to verify whether almost $229,000 in taxpayer dollars spent on such projects were properly accounted for.

Investigators only inspected four humanitarian assistance worksites—two in Djibouti and two in Tanzania—but even in this tiny sample found one site where the United States military had failed to ensure that the host nation would sustain the project. At the Ali Sabieh Community Water Fountains in Djibouti, renovated by the United States in 2010 to minimize waterborne disease, investigators found a scene of utter disrepair. Doors, pipes, and faucets "had been removed," while another faucet "had a collapsed top," leaving the water "exposed to contaminants." Photographs taken two years after the project was completed display dilapidated, crumbling, and seemingly jerry-rigged structures.

One American official assured inspector general investigators of the necessity of obtaining host nation "buy-in" on such projects to achieve success, while another suggested it was crucial that local "sweat equity" be invested in such projects, if they weren't to become "monuments to U.S. failure." In Djibouti, however, local residents were apparently given no information about upkeep of the Ali Sabieh project. As a result, Djiboutians threw rocks into a well built by Americans, a method that works to raise water in indigenously built wells. In this case, however, it damaged the well so badly that it stopped working.

Examining a sample of projects, the Pentagon's investigators found that 73 percent of the time CJTF-HOA personnel failed to collect sufficient data thirty days after completion of projects, to assess whether it achieved the stated objectives. For example, at a medical clinic at Manza Bay, the United States built cisterns and a water catchment system. The project was apparently considered a success, but the military had very little data to back up that claim. In Garissa, in neighboring Kenya, a veterinary civic action project was evidently also declared a triumph without anything to prove it beyond vague upbeat claims of success in impressing local residents.

Winning Hearts and Minds
or Losing Money and Influence?

After reviewing a draft of the inspector general's report last year, AFRICOM Chief of Staff Nickle offered a response clearly meant to undermine the Pentagon watchdog's claims. In his September 2013 memorandum, Nickle took particular issue with the inspector general's investigative methodology, decrying its lack of statistical sampling. Since the report is restricted, the inspector general's office refused to discuss the specifics of its analysis with TomDispatch, but Brenda Rolin of its Office of Communications and Congressional Liaison defended the methodology. Nonstatistical sampling, she explained, "can be used to obtain sufficient audit evidence. This method is valid but results may not be projected to the entire population." Nickle also complained that the inspector general's team did not include an expert familiar with all the types of humanitarian efforts AFRICOM carried out and that the investigators failed to highlight its successes.

Nearly a year has passed since the drafting of the inspector general's report. During that time, neither AFRICOM nor CJTF-HOA has publicly addressed it or announced any changes based on its recommendations. In the meantime, the hearts and minds of allied African military leaders appear unswayed by AFRICOM's efforts. Over two days at the Land Forces East Africa conference in Dar es Salaam, I listened to generals and defense analysts from around the region speak on security matters affecting Burundi, Kenya, Somalia, Uganda, and Tanzania. They touched on the key issues—extremism, terrorism, and piracy—that the American hearts-and-minds campaign is meant to counter, but the United States was hardly mentioned. Tanzanian officers I talked with, for instance, were pleased to be receiving American funds, but less so with direct US interventions of any type on the continent. None I spoke with seemed aware of AFRICOM'S hearts-and-minds work like clean water projects or school construction in underdeveloped rural areas not so very far from where we've been sitting.

Even Egan O'Reilly, an army officer attached to the US Embassy here, whose job is to facilitate "security cooperation" activities, had little idea about AFRICOM's humanitarian efforts.

Dual-hatted—answering to the US ambassador in Tanzania and AFRICOM—he's new to the mission but high on America's efforts in the region. "We've done everything from helping bring down trainers for military intelligence courses to building their own schoolhouse for intelligence work," he tells me.

What about the building of primary and secondary schools, the humanitarian assistance projects? "I haven't seen a whole lot of AFRICOM work myself," replies the West Point graduate and veteran of the wars in Iraq and Afghanistan. As O'Reilly told me, he had heard about the work of the Medical Civil Action Program, or MEDCAP—meant to provide medical care or increase local medical capacity in underserved areas—but that was about it. And while such programs are "good and they make people smile," he adds, they're of limited utility. Logistics training and engineering instruction for African militaries, that's "the important stuff."

TomDispatch also sought interviews with US defense attachés in Ethiopia, Djibouti, and Kenya for assessments of the humanitarian projects in those respective countries. The latter two embassies failed to respond to the requests, while a spokesperson for the US mission in Ethiopia thanked me for my interest but told me that the defense attaché "is not currently available for an interview." No one, it appears, is eager to talk about the textbook counterinsurgency campaign being carried out by the US military in Africa, let alone the failures chronicled in an inspector general report that's been withheld from the public for almost a year.

For the past decade, we've been inundated with disclosures about billions of US tax dollars squandered on counterinsurgency failures in Iraq and Afghanistan, stories of ruined roads and busted buildings, shoddy schoolhouses and wasteful water parks, all in the name of winning hearts and minds. Below the radar, similar—

if smaller scale—efforts are well under way in Africa. Already, the schools are being built, already the water projects are falling to pieces, already the Department of Defense's inspector general has identified a plethora of problems. It's just been kept under wraps. But if history is any guide, humanitarian efforts by AFRICOM and CJTF-HOA will grow larger and ever more expensive, until they join the long list of projects that have become "monuments to US failure" around the world.

12

American "Success" and the Rise of West African Piracy: Pirates of the Gulf of Guinea

September 25, 2014

"The Gulf of Guinea is the most insecure waterway, globally," says Loic Moudouma. And he should know. Trained at the US Naval War College, the lead maritime security expert of the Economic Community of Central African States, and a Gabonese Navy commander, his focus has been piracy and maritime crime in the region for the better part of a decade.

Moudouma is hardly alone in his assessment.

From 2012 to 2013, the US Office of Naval Intelligence found a 25 percent jump in incidents, including vessels being fired upon, boarded, and hijacked, in the Gulf of Guinea, a vast maritime zone that curves along the west coast of Africa from Gabon to Liberia. Kidnappings are up, too. Stephen Starr, writing for the *CTC Sentinel*, the official publication of the Combating Terrorism

Center at West Point, asserted that in 2014, the number of attacks would rise again.

Today, what most Americans know about piracy likely centers on an attraction at Walt Disney World and the Johnny Depp movies it inspired. If the Gulf of Guinea rings any bells at all, it's probably because of the Ebola outbreak in and US military-medical "surge" into Liberia, the nation on the northern edge of that body of water. But for those in the know, the Gulf itself is an intractable hotspot on a vast continent filled with them and yet another area where US military efforts have fallen short.

A recent investigation by the US Government Accountability Office (GAO) found that "piracy and maritime crime in the Gulf of Guinea has escalated" and that "armed robbery at sea, oil theft, and kidnapping is a persistent problem that continues to contribute to instability" there. Not only that, but as Pottengal Mukundan, the director of the International Maritime Bureau of the International Chamber of Commerce, recently noted, piracy in the gulf has taken on a particularly violent character.

What AFRICOM'S Benson thinks isn't quite so clear. As the situation in the Gulf of Guinea was worsening, he touted it as an American "success" story, pure and simple. Then he claimed that he hadn't done so, after which he clammed up completely. What he thinks today is anyone's guess. He refuses to say a word about it.

Moudouma, for his part, claims to see progress in bringing security to a body of water nearly the size of the Gulf of Mexico that is critical to the economies of a dozen nations. He also credits the United States for its support of security efforts there, even if they have paradoxically occurred alongside an increase in both piracy and insecurity. West African states, says Moudouma, have left waterways ungoverned, turning them into breeding grounds for criminal activity. The problem, he insists, is the poor leadership of the African nations in the region, America's "partners" on the frontlines of the fight. Their lust for power, according to Moudouma, has put the national security of numerous African nations and the economic well-being of the region at risk, yet in Washington in August 2014, the Obama administration feted the area's most corrupt strongman and the US military regularly partners with his armed forces.

The Sweet Smell of Success

"Do not put words in my mouth. I did not say the Gulf of Guinea was a success. I did not say Gulf of Guinea maritime security was a success." This was AFRICOM spokesman Benson's response in November 2013 when I asked if he wanted to amend his earlier assessment of the Gulf of Guinea shortly after pirates kidnapped two Americans from a US-flagged ship there.

I was taken aback.

I remembered him touting the region as a triumph when we talked in the spring of that year, so I went back to a recording of our conversation. "I'm wondering what you think the big success stories are," I had asked about AFRICOM's work on the continent. "There's actually two success stories," he replied, telling me first about American efforts in Somalia. "Another area that's definitely a success is the Gulf of Guinea," he added. "We've been working with a number of different states developing . . . maritime security capabilities."

I listened to that passage several times. It sure sounded like he was calling the Gulf of Guinea a success.

For almost a year since then, Benson has failed to amend, clarify, or defend his statement. He had ignored repeated requests for further information, refusing even to issue a pro forma "no

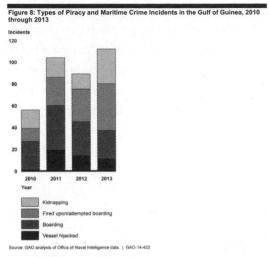

Figure 8: Types of Piracy and Maritime Crime Incidents in the Gulf of Guinea, 2010 through 2013

Source: GAO analysis of Office of Naval Intelligence data. | GAO-14-422

Analysis of Office of Naval Intelligence data by the Government Account-ability Office from "Ongoing U.S. Counter-piracy Efforts Would Benefit from Agency Assessments" (GAO 14-422).

comment." He may still claim that he never uttered those words or he may still believe the gulf has been an American success story, but even his boss, General David Rodriguez, in testimony before the House Armed Services Committee earlier this year, said "maritime criminal activities in the Gulf of Guinea remain at concerning levels."

America's Battle Against Pirates

The United States has been fighting African pirates since the early days of the republic—battles so formative that, among other things, they established a long-standing pattern of dealing with foreign policy problems through armed interventions and also inspired the iconic phrase "the shores of Tripoli" in the Marine Corps hymn. By the late 2000s, American ships were once again under attack off an African coastline and the U.S. military had again been dispatched to kill pirates. This time around, the conflict centered on the Horn of Africa—not North Africa—specifically the waters off the coast of Somalia.

In the 1990s, Somalia descended into a maelstrom of violence, which has abated somewhat in recent years but continues to plague that nation and has since spread beyond its borders. In 1993, when American troops infamously arrived in its capital, Mogadishu, in support of a United Nations humanitarian mission, they suffered eighteen killed and two helicopters shot out of the sky in the "Black Hawk Down" disaster. Somalia was then repeatedly battered as Islamic militants struggled for control against US-backed militias and various African armed forces. During those years, neighboring nations began illegally fishing in Somali waters, prompting local fishermen to arm themselves and collect "taxes" from foreign vessels. Some of these proto-pirates soon began hijacking relief food shipments, while others moved on to attacking merchant vessels and oil tankers. By 2008, Somali swashbucklers were, by some estimates, raking in as much as $150 million annually.

That same year, the US National Security Council (NSC) developed a document it called "Countering Piracy off the Horn of Africa: Partnership and Action Plan." Its focus was the prevention and disruption of maritime crime off the coast of Somalia. Despite this, the number of reported attacks in the region nearly doubled between 2008 and 2009, and the next year the GAO weighed in with recommendations for the NSC to "reassess and update its Action Plan; identify metrics; assess the costs, benefits, and effectiveness of U.S. counter-piracy activities; and clarify agency roles and responsibilities." For the next four years, however, the NSC failed to respond.

In those years, the United Nations also passed numerous resolutions related to maritime crime in the Horn of Africa, authorizing international militaries to conduct counterpiracy efforts. Naval patrols and other missions by NATO and the European Union as well as Australia, Bahrain, Canada, France, Jordan, South Korea, the Netherlands, Pakistan, Saudi Arabia, Singapore, Spain, Thailand, Turkey, China, Russia, Japan, India, and the United States—in addition to the use of armed mercenaries to protect ships and a slew of new policies designed to thwart attacks—have had a demonstrable effect. According to the International Maritime Bureau, piracy incidents in the Horn of Africa declined from 219 in 2010 to just 15 in 2013.

"At the peak point of operations, up to thirty vessels from as many as twenty-two nations were engaged in counter-piracy operations in the region," Rear Admiral Joseph Kuzmick told Congress last year. "International naval forces have thwarted pirate attacks in progress, engaged pirate skiffs, and successfully taken back hijacked ships during opposed boardings." While a truly international effort, the battle against the Somali pirates ranks as one of the few bright spots for the US military in Africa.

Over these same years, the United States has also been pouring money and effort into maritime security activities on the other side of the continent with drastically different results.

From 2007 to 2011, the United States provided $35 million to West and Central African countries for coastal radar, boats, equipment, and maritime security training. These efforts included the African Partnership Station (APS)—a shipboard effort designed to "provide quality military training to sailors and leaders of [partner] nations." Under the auspices of the APS, the United States annually hosts four regional security exercises around the African continent: Cutlass Express, Phoenix Express, Saharan

Gulf of Guinea (April 2, 2014). US sailors, US Coast Guardsmen, and Ghanaian maritime specialists, ride in a rigid-hull inflatable boat as part of a US-Ghana combined maritime law enforcement operation under the African Maritime Law Enforcement Partnership program. (US Navy photo by Mass Communication Specialist 2nd Class Jeff Atherton)

Express, and Obangame Express, the latter based in the waters off West Africa.

By 2012, APS activities involved more than thirty African, European, and North and South American countries. In last year's iteration of Obangame Express, some sixteen nations participated in exercises in the Gulf of Guinea, including Benin, Cameroon, Côte d'Ivoire, Equatorial Guinea, France, Gabon, Nigeria, Republic of Congo, São Tomé and Príncipe, Togo, and the United States. This year, twenty nations were involved, including eleven which took part in boarding exercises conducted aboard thirty-six different vessels in the gulf.

AFRICOM and the US Coast Guard also provide counter-piracy training as well as instruction in search and seizure skills through the African Maritime Law Enforcement Partnership program. In addition, the United States has held seminars, symposiums, and conferences devoted to maritime security; it has donated spare parts and even entire ships to West African allies, provided hands-on maintenance instruction; advised personnel from regional navies and coast guards; and offered aid for maritime counter-narcotics and law-enforcement projects.

Despite all these efforts, maritime insecurity has been markedly on the rise in the waters off West Africa. When I spoke last year with AFRICOM's Benson about signs of US "success" in the Gulf of Guinea, he cited US efforts that culminated in a conference where West and Central African leaders would hammer out a comprehensive strategy to improve maritime security, with a formal code of conduct for states to follow. At the time, however, the conference—organized by the Economic Community of Central African States, the Economic Community of West African States, and the Commission of the Gulf of Guinea—had yet to take place.

How could that count as a success, I wondered, especially when signs of regional failure were all too evident? According to the US Office of Naval Intelligence, incidents of piracy and maritime crime in the Gulf of Guinea jumped more than 80 percent from 2010 to 2013. According to Oceans Beyond Piracy, an advocacy group focusing on maritime security issues, West African pirates attacked at least 1,871 "seafarers" in 2013, and 279 were known to have been taken hostage. Additionally, 1,209 vessels were boarded by pirates. Experts now estimate that $2 billion is lost each year in port revenue, insurance premiums, and security costs due to maritime crime in the Gulf of Guinea.

Getting Cozy with Africa's Most Corrupt Strongman

It was at a conference hosted by the Department of Defense's Africa Center for Strategic Studies, held on the periphery of the

White House's US-Africa Leaders Summit in August 2014, that Moudouma spoke positively about US assistance in the region while also asserting that the Gulf of Guinea was the most insecure and violent waterway in the entire world. When I questioned him about this apparent paradox—asking why maritime insecurity has escalated during years of increased US assistance—he pointed to the slow pace in implementing plans and the relentlessness of the region's pirates. He also put the blame squarely on America's allies in Africa. "The state is still absent from the sea," he said, drawing attention to the inability of nations to police their territorial waters. Moudouma also called out the region's heads of state. "Over the last decade, our political leaders have been investing in how to stay in power as long as possible," he said.

Moudouma sees systemic problems at the ministerial and presidential levels in African governments and called for more action aimed at heads of state. This type of pressure, however, didn't seem to be on the table at that White House summit when President Obama hosted—and stood for a smiling portrait with—Equatorial Guinea's President Teodoro Obiang.

Since he first seized power in a coup thirty-five years ago (just before Obama began his freshman year in college), Obiang has ruled that tiny, oil-rich nation on the Gulf of Guinea with an iron fist. A perennial pariah state, his country is noted for its utter lack of press freedom and political opposition, and a profusion of corruption, oppression, and human rights abuses, including extrajudicial killings and the imprisonment and torture of opposition figures. While most of Equatorial Guinea lives on about $2 a day, the Obiang family lives the high life, complete with a fleet of flashy cars—including Ferraris, Rolls-Royces, and Lamborghinis—not to mention private jets.

The country seems to be the archetypal example of the sort of corruption Moudouma denounced. It ranked 163 out of 175 on Transparency International's Corruption Perceptions Index in 2013. Yet year after year, US forces have partnered with those of Equatorial Guinea for military exercises, training missions, and even, according to a 2009 navy press release, "a flight deck reception for distinguished Equatorial Guinean visitors in order to develop relationships and promote regional cooperation between Equatorial Guinea and the United States."

Succeeding at Failure

On June 19, 2014, the Government Accountability Office published a new report, "Ongoing U.S. Counter-Piracy Efforts Would Benefit from Agency Assessments." It contrasted the much-improved situation off Somalia's coast with the "persistent problem" of piracy and maritime crime in the Gulf of Guinea. It also drew attention to recommendations—like systematically tracking costs and identifying which agencies will lead or support various counterpiracy efforts—that, after four years, had yet to be implemented.

A day later, the National Security Council (NSC) unveiled its 2014 "United States Counter Piracy and Maritime Security Action Plan." According to a statement provided to TomDispatch by NSC spokesman Ned Price, it "provides guidance to the Federal government focusing on three core areas including: prevention of attacks, response to acts of maritime crime, and enhancing maritime security and governance."

The new plan contains an annex devoted to the Gulf of Guinea (which went unmentioned in the 2008 report) and, according to the NSC, "effectively addresses the recommendations raised in the [June 2014 GAO] report." That isn't quite the case according to Stephen

Caldwell, one of that report's authors. "Our recommendations from the earlier report were only partially fulfilled," he told me. "Some of the more specific issues were not addressed."

While acknowledging that the NSC has a lot on its plate beyond piracy, Caldwell drew attention to the ways in which a continuing failure to track costs, identify resource constraints, and define specific roles for the agencies involved in maritime security efforts can lead to a lack of accountability and the inability to fix ineffective efforts. "Although the United States has interagency and international efforts underway with African states to strengthen maritime security, it has not assessed its efforts or the need for a collective plan to address the evolving problem in the region," says the GAO report. "The U.S. role in addressing piracy in the Gulf of Guinea has focused on prevention, disruption, and prosecution, through training and assistance to African coastal states. However, according to U.S. agencies working in the region, the National Security Council Staff (NSCS) has not directed them to collectively assess their efforts to address piracy and maritime crime."

US failures when it comes to the Gulf of Guinea are many: a failure to address the long-standing concerns of a government watchdog agency, a failure to effectively combat piracy despite an outlay of tens of millions of taxpayer dollars, and a failure to confront corrupt African leaders who enable piracy in the first place. In fact, the rolling out of a red carpet in Washington for an astoundingly corrupt West African strongman, precisely the type of leader even a Pentagon-approved analyst cites as the source of regional instability, mirrors other US efforts in Africa, from Libya to Mali to South Sudan, which have crumbled, collapsed, crashed, and burned.

For the better part of a year, following his email outburst about putting words in his mouth, US Africa Command spokesman Benjamin Benson has ignored my repeated requests for comment or clarification when it comes to the Gulf of Guinea. And it's little wonder. After all, as the US military has shown repeatedly in its "pivot" to Africa over these last years, it's so much easier to claim success than to achieve it.

13

The Outpost That Doesn't Exist in the Country You Can't Locate: A Base Camp, an Authoritarian Regime, and the Future of US Blowback in Africa

November 20, 2014

Admit it. You don't know where Chad is. You know it's in Africa, of course. But beyond that? Maybe with a map of the continent and by some process of elimination you could come close. But you'd probably pick Sudan or maybe the Central African Republic. Here's a tip. In the future, choose that vast, arid swath of land just below Libya.

Who does know where Chad is? That answer is simpler: the US military. Contracting documents from late 2014 indicate that it's building something there. Not a huge facility, not a mini-American town, but a small camp.

That the US military is expanding its efforts in Africa shouldn't be a shock anymore. For years, the Pentagon has been promoting a mini-basing boom that has left it with a growing collection of outposts across the northern tier of the continent. This string of camps is meant to do what a decade-plus of counterterrorism efforts has failed to accomplish: transform the trans-Sahara region in the northern and western parts of the continent into a bulwark of stability.

That the United States is doing more in Chad specifically isn't particularly astonishing. In early 2014, TomDispatch and the *Washington Post* both reported on separate deployments of US troops to that north-central African nation. Nor is it shocking that the new American compound is to be located near the capital, N'Djamena. The United States has previously employed N'Djamena as a hub for its air operations. What's striking is the terminology used in the official documents. After years of adamant claims that the US military has just one lonely base in all of Africa—Camp Lemonnier in Djibouti—army documents state that it will now have "base camp facilities" in Chad.

US Africa Command (AFRICOM) still insists that there is no Chadian base, that the camp serves only as temporary lodgings to support a Special Operations training exercise to be held in 2015. It also refused to comment about another troop deployment to Chad uncovered by TomDispatch. When it comes to American military activities in Africa, much remains murky.

Nonetheless, one fact is crystal clear: the United States is ever more tied to Chad. This remains true despite a decade-long effort to train its military forces only to see them bolt from one mission in the face of casualties, leave another in a huff after gunning down unarmed civilians, and engage in human rights abuses at home with utter impunity. All of this suggests yet another potential source of blowback from America's efforts in Africa which have backfired, gone bust, and sown strife from Libya to South Sudan, the Gulf Guinea to Mali, and beyond.

A Checkered History with Chad

Following 9/11, the United States launched the Pan-Sahel Initiative to bolster the militaries of Mali, Niger, Mauritania, and Chad. Three years later, the program expanded to include Nigeria, Senegal, Morocco, Algeria, and Tunisia as the Trans-Sahara Counterterrorism Partnership (TSCTP). The idea was to turn a huge swath of Africa into a terror-resistant bulwark of stability. Twelve years and hundreds of millions of dollars later, the region is anything but stable, which means that it fits like a missing puzzle piece with the rest of the under-the-radar US pivot to that continent.

Coups by the US-backed militaries of Mauritania in 2005 and again in 2008, Niger in 2010, and Mali in 2012, as well as a 2011 revolution that overthrew Tunisia's US-backed government (after the U.S.-supported army stood aside); the establishment of al-Qaeda in the Islamic Maghreb in 2006; and the rise of Boko Haram from an obscure radical sect to a raging insurgent movement in northern Nigeria are only some of the most notable recent failures in TSCTP nations. Chad came close to making the list, too, but attempted military coups in 2006 and 2013 were thwarted, and in 2008, the government, which had itself come to power in a 1990 coup, managed to hold off a rebel assault on the capital.

Through it all, the United States has continued to mentor Chad's military, and in return, that nation has lent its muscle to support Washington's interests in the region. Chad, for instance, joined the 2013 U.S.-backed French military intervention to retake Mali after Islamists began routing the forces of the American-trained officer who had launched a coup that overthrew that country's democratically elected government. According to military briefing slides obtained by TomDispatch, an Intelligence, Surveillance, and Reconnaissance (ISR) liaison team was deployed to Chad to aid operations in Mali and the United States also conducted pre-deployment training for its Chadian proxies. After initial success, the French effort bogged down and has now become a seemingly interminable, smoldering counterinsurgency campaign. Chad, for its part, quickly withdrew its forces from the fight after sustaining modest casualties. "Chad's army has no ability to face the kind of guerrilla fighting that is emerging in northern Mali. Our soldiers are going to return to Chad," said that country's president, Idriss Deby.

Still, US support continued.

In September 2013, the US military organized meetings with Chad's senior-most military leaders, including army chief General Ibrahim Seid Mahamat, Minister of Defense General Béna-indo Tatola, and counterterror tsar Brigadier General Abderaman Youssouf Merry, to solidify relationships and support efforts at "countering violent extremist operations objectives and theater security cooperation programs." This comes from a separate set of documents concerning IO, or Information Operations, obtained from the military through the Freedom of Information Act. French officials also attended these meetings and the agenda included the former colonial power's support of "security cooperation with Chad in the areas of basic and officer training and staff procedures" as well as "French support [for] U.S. security cooperation efforts with the Chadian military." Official briefing slides also mention ongoing "train and equip" activities with Chadian troops.

All of this followed on the heels of a murky coup plot by elements of the armed forces last May to which the Chadian military reacted with a crescendo of violence. According to a State Department report, Chad's "security forces shot and killed unarmed civilians and arrested and detained members of parliament, military officers, former rebels, and others."

After Chad reportedly helped overthrow the Central African Republic's president in early 2013 and later aided in the 2014 ouster of the rebel leader who deposed him, it sent its forces into that civil war–torn land as part of an African Union mission bolstered by U.S.-backed French troops. Soon, Chad's peacekeeping forces were accused of stoking sectarian strife by supporting Muslim militias against Christian fighters. Then, on March 29, a Chadian military convoy arrived in a crowded marketplace in the capital, Bangui. There, according to a United Nations report, the troops "reportedly opened fire on the population without any provocation. At the time, the market was full of people, including many girls and women buying and selling produce. As panic-stricken people fled in all directions, the soldiers allegedly continued firing indiscriminately."

In all, thirty civilians were reportedly killed and more than three hundred were wounded. Amid criticism, Chad angrily announced that it was withdrawing its troops. "Despite the sacrifices we have made, Chad and Chadians have been targeted in a gratuitous and malicious campaign that blamed them for all the suffering" in the Central African Republic, declared Chad's foreign ministry.

In May 2014, despite this, the United States sent eighty military personnel to Chad to operate drones and conduct surveillance in an effort to locate hundreds of schoolgirls kidnapped by Boko Haram in neighboring Nigeria. "These personnel will support the operation of intelligence, surveillance, and reconnaissance aircraft for missions over northern Nigeria and the surrounding area,"

President Obama told Congress. The force, he said, will remain in Chad "until its support in resolving the kidnapping situation is no longer required."

That July, AFRICOM admitted that it had reduced surveillance flights searching for the girls to focus on other missions. In November, AFRICOM told TomDispatch that, while "the U.S. continues to help Nigeria address the threat posed by Boko Haram, the previously announced ISR support deployment to Chad has departed." Yet more than seven months after their abduction, the girls still had not been located, let alone rescued.

In June 2014, according to the State Department, the deputy commander of US Army Africa (USARAF), Brigadier General Kenneth H. Moore Jr., visited Chad to "celebrat[e] the successful conclusion of a partnership between USARAF and the Chadian Armed Forces." Secretary of the Navy Ray Mabus arrived in that landlocked country at the same time to meet with "top Chadian officials." His visit, according to an embassy press release, "underscore[d] the importance of bilateral relations between the two countries, as well as military cooperation." And that cooperation has been ample.

Chadian troops joined those of the United States, Burkina Faso, Canada, France, Mauritania, the Netherlands, Nigeria, Senegal, the United Kingdom, and host nation Niger for three weeks of military drills as part of Flintlock 2014, an annual Special Ops counterterrorism exercise for TSCTP nations. At about the time Flintlock was concluding, soldiers from Chad, Cameroon, Burundi, Gabon, Nigeria, the Republic of Congo, the Netherlands, and the United States took part in another annual training exercise, Central Accord 2014. The army also sent medical personnel to mentor Chadian counterparts in "tactical combat casualty care," while marines and navy personnel traveled to Chad to train that country's militarized anti-poaching park rangers in small unit tactics and patrolling.

A separate contingent of Marines conducted military intelligence training with Chadian officers and noncommissioned officers. The scenario for the final exercise, also involving personnel from Burkina Faso, Cameroon, Mauritania, Senegal, and Tunisia, had a ripped-from-the-headlines quality: "preparing for an unconventional war against an insurgent threat in Mali."

As for US Army Africa, it sent trainers as part of a separate effort to provide Chadian troops with instruction on patrolling and fixed-site defense as well as live-fire training. "We are ready to begin training in Chad for about 1,300 soldiers—an 850-man battalion, plus another 450 man battalion," said Colonel John Ruffing, the Security Cooperation director of US Army Africa, noting that the United States was working in tandem with a French private security firm.

In September 2014, AFRICOM reaffirmed its close ties with Chad by renewing an Acquisition Cross Servicing Agreement, which allows both militaries to purchase from each other or trade for basic supplies. The open-ended pact, said Brigadier General James Vechery, AFRICOM's director for logistics, "will continue to strengthen our bilateral cooperation on international security issues . . . as well as the interoperability of the armed forces of both nations."

The Base That Wasn't
and the Deployment That Might Be

In the months after the Chadian armed forces' March 2014 massacre in Bangui, various US military contract solicitations and related documents pointed toward an even more substantive American presence in Chad. In late September of that year, the army put out a call for bids to sustain American personnel for six months at those "base camp facilities" located near N'Djamena. Supporting documents specifically mention thirty-five US personnel and detail the services necessary to run an austere outpost: field sanitation, bulk water supply, sewage services, and trash removal. The materials indicate that "local security policy and procedures" are to be provided by the Chadian armed forces and allude to the use of more than one location, saying "none of the sites in Chad are considered U.S.-federally controlled facilities." The documents state that such support for those facilities is to run until July 2015.

After AFRICOM failed to respond to repeated email requests for further information, I called up Chief of Media Operations Benjamin Benson and asked about the base camp. He was even more tight-lipped than usual. "I personally don't know anything," he told me. "That's not saying AFRICOM doesn't have any information on that."

In follow-up emails, Benson eventually told me that the "base camp" is strictly a temporary facility to be used by US forces only for the duration of the upcoming Flintlock 2015 exercise. He stated in no uncertain terms: "We are not establishing a base/forward presence/contingency location, building a U.S. facility, or stationing troops in Chad."

Benson would not, however, allow me to speak with an expert on US military activities in Chad. Nor would he confirm or deny the continued presence of the ISR liaison team deployed to Chad in 2013 to support the French mission in Mali, first reported on by TomDispatch in March 2014. "We cannot discuss ISR activities or the locations and durations of operational deployments," he wrote. If an ISR team is still present in Chad, this would represent a substantive long-term deployment despite the lack of a formal US base.

The N'Djamena "base camp" is just one of a series of Chadian projects mentioned in recent contracting documents. An army solicitation from September 2014 sought "building materials for use in Chad," while supporting documents specifically mentioned an "operations center/multi-use facility." That same month, the army awarded a contract for the transport of equipment from Niamey, Niger, the home of another in the growing network of US outposts in Africa, to N'Djamena. The army also began seeking out contractors capable of supplying close to 600 bunk beds that could support an American-sized weight of 200 to 225 pounds for a facility "in and around the N'Djamena region." And in October, the military put out a call for a contractor to supply construction equipment—a bulldozer, dump truck, excavator, and the like—for a project in, you guessed it, N'Djamena.

This increased US interest in Chad follows on the heels of a push by France, the nation's former colonial overlord and America's current premier proxy in Africa, to beef up its military footprint on the continent. In July 2014, following US-backed French military interventions in Mali and the Central African Republic, French President François Hollande announced a new mission, Operation Barkhane (a term for a crescent-shaped sand dune found in the Sahara). Its purpose: a long-term counterterrorism mission involving 3,000 French troops deployed to a special forces outpost in Burkina Faso and forward operating bases in Mali, Niger, and not surprisingly, Chad.

"There are plenty of threats in all directions," Hollande told French soldiers in Chad, citing militants in Mali and Libya as well as Boko Haram in Nigeria. "Rather than having large bases that are difficult to manage in moments of crisis, we prefer installations that can be used quickly and efficiently." Shortly afterward, President Obama approved millions in emergency military aid for French operations in Mali, Niger, and Chad, while the United

Kingdom, another former colonial power in the region, dispatched combat aircraft to the French base in N'Djamena to contribute to the battle against Boko Haram.

From Setback to Blowback?

In recent years, the US military has been involved in a continual process of expanding its presence in Africa. Out of public earshot, officials have talked about setting up a string of small bases across the northern tier of the continent. Indeed, over the past years, US staging areas, mini-bases, and outposts have popped up in the contiguous nations of Senegal, Mali, Burkina Faso, Niger, and, skipping Chad, in the Central African Republic, followed by South Sudan, Uganda, Kenya, Ethiopia, and Djibouti. A staunch American ally with a frequent and perhaps enduring American troop presence, Chad seems like the natural spot for still another military compound—the only missing link in a long chain of countries stretching from west to east, from one edge of the continent to the other—even if AFRICOM continues to insist that there's no American "base" in the works.

Even without a base, the United States has for more than a decade poured copious amounts of money, time, and effort into making Chad a stable regional counterterrorism partner, sending troops there, training and equipping its army, counseling its military leaders, providing tens of millions of dollars in aid, funding its military expeditions, supplying its army with equipment ranging from tents to trucks, donating additional equipment for its domestic security forces, providing a surveillance and security system for its border security agents, and looking the other way when its military employed child soldiers.

The results? A flight from the fight in Mali, a massacre in

the Central African Republic, hundreds of schoolgirls still in the clutches of Boko Haram, and a US alliance with a regime whose "most significant human rights problems," according to the most recent country report by the State Department's Bureau of Democracy, Human Rights, and Labor, "were security force abuse, including torture; harsh prison conditions; and discrimination and violence against women and children," not to mention the restriction of freedom of speech, press, assembly, and movement, as well as arbitrary arrest and detention, denial of fair public trial, executive influence on the judiciary, property seizures, child labor and forced labor (that also includes children), among other abuses. Amnesty International further found that human rights violations "are committed with almost total impunity" by members of the Chadian military, the Presidential Guard, and the state intelligence bureau, the Agence Nationale de Securité.

With Chad, the United States finds itself more deeply involved with yet another authoritarian government and another atrocity-prone proxy force. In this, it continues a long series of mistakes, missteps, and mishaps across Africa. These include an intervention in Libya that transformed the country from an autocracy into a near-failed state, training efforts that produced coup leaders in Mali and Burkina Faso, American nation-building that led to a failed state in South Sudan, anti-piracy measures that flopped in the Gulf of Guinea, the many fiascos of the Trans-Sahara Counterterrorism Partnership, the training of an elite Congolese unit that committed mass rapes and other atrocities, problem-plagued humanitarian efforts in Djibouti and Ethiopia, and the steady rise of terror groups in US-backed countries like Nigeria and Tunisia.

In other words, in its shadowy pivot to Africa, the U.S. military has compiled a record remarkably low on successes and high on blowback. Is it time to add Chad to this growing list?

Finding Barack Obama in South Sudan

JUBA, South Sudan. The camp is a mess of orange muck and open earthen sewers. A single wood plank provides passage over a roughhewn trench. Children peek out from tarp-tents. Older men and women sit in homes of mud-speckled plastic sheeting that become saunas in the midday heat. Young women pick their way through refuse, some with large yellow jerry cans of water balanced atop their heads, others carry their homes in similar fashion—a mess of wooden poles and a folded tarp—as they set out for another camp hoping for better to come.

As I walk down the main thoroughfare of this camp for internal exiles, I suddenly see his smiling face, the one I'd know anywhere. Here, in Juba, the capital of South Sudan amid tens of thousands of people crammed into a fetid encampment visibly thrown together in haste, out of fear and necessity; here, as huge water tanker trucks rumble past and men in camouflage fatigues, toting automatic weapons, stride by; here, in the unlikeliest of places, in the heat and swirling dust and charcoal smoke, the air heavy with the scent of squalor, is a face I've seen a thousand, or ten thousand, or a million times before. Here in a camp where hopelessness is endemic and despair reigns, is a face that, for so many, was once synonymous with hope itself. It's a sight that stops me in my tracks. Here, 7,000 miles from my home, Barack Obama is smiling his familiar smile amid the results of a decades-long American project in Africa.

"It was George Bush and the Christian fundamentalists who heard the cry of South Sudan," Taban Lo Liyong, a South Sudanese writer and literature professor at the University of Juba, told the *Los Angeles Times* a day after his country's independence in 2011. "Today is Barack Obama's day. We don't know what he is going to do."

Only three years ago, the future seemed wide open and *hope* was the operative word. In fact, all the nation could do then was hope—and dream of better to come.

Dreams and Nightmares

"My dream," Giel says when I ask about his red T-shirt, which sports a picture of President Obama's smiling face in front of an American flag. Indeed, the shirt reads: "Obama: My Dream."

Just what that dream is, however, couldn't, at this point, be murkier.

When I run into Giel in this squalid United Nations camp, he's already been living here for more than six months. After fighting broke out in December 2013, he tells me, Dinka soldiers from South Sudan's army killed his uncle. Neighbors died, too. Indeed, hundreds of men from his tribe, the Nuers, were killed in his Juba neighborhood, while Dinka civilians suffered the price of payback elsewhere in the country. "It's not safe to go home," says the fourteen-year-old. "I fear we will be killed." And so he sits, day after day, for eight to ten hours, at a little stand—a white plastic table under a blue umbrella—on the camp's main drag, selling bags of bread.

Home for the nine members of Giel's family sheltering in this camp is a plastic tent. There's never enough food, he tells me, there are hardly any jobs, and it's stiflingly hot. When it rains, the camp turns into a sea of mud, you can't sleep, you can't do much at all. It's a metaphor for his country—not that South Sudan needs any metaphors, given the reality at hand. It's been paralyzed for a year by simmering conflict. "South Sudan has very big problems because of the war," he says matter of factly.

Deeper into the camp, making my way through a warren of makeshift shanties, tents, and other kinds of homes constructed from tarps and blankets, I call upon Nyadoang. Her cheeks are sunken and her long legs are rail thin. She might be in her twenties, but appears older, weary, world-worn. She doesn't know her own age. Her twins are four years old. The naked baby boy that she's alternately breast-feeding and gently jiggling in her hands as if he were a hot potato, was born just a few months before in the dirt floor hovel that is now their home, a tangle of hanging fabric and wooden support poles encased in plastic tarps.

Nyadoang wears a blouse of radiant pink and orange that catches the eye in this bleak setting, but she looks defeated. And with good reason. She fled to the camp when the fighting started and has been stranded here ever since, separated from her husband. Her fractured family seems emblematic of so much in this fractured "nation." Her twins were born in Sudan in 2010, became South Sudanese the next year, and now find themselves trapped in a camp for internal exiles in a country trapped in a civil war limbo. Her newborn son has never known any other life. A local woman, an employee of the International Rescue Committee, a nongovernmental organization working in the camp, caught the mood of the moment perfectly when she told me, "We were born refugees. Some of our children are now born refugees. It's really traumatizing. We need a permanent solution."

But solutions to even basic problems here seem to be in short supply. Nyadoang says she can't get baby formula and her newborn has a cough, fever, and diarrhea. There are no jobs in the camp and even if there were, who would watch the baby? There's no money to be had and no end in sight. Trust between the Nuer and Dinka has broken down. Even personal friendships have snapped under the weight of the crisis, she tells me. "How can we live a normal life while the war goes on?"

What does she want for her children, what type of future does she hope for in South Sudan? "We can't go back home if there's no peace," she tells me. "Maybe there is no future."

This is the legacy of America's nation-building project in Africa, and of the policies of a president born of an African father, a president whose name was once synonymous with hope for the future.

Over the course of the Obama presidency, American efforts on the continent have become ever more militarized in terms of troops and bases, missions and money. And yet from Libya to the Gulf of Guinea, Mali to this camp in South Sudan, the results have been dismal. Countless military exercises, counterterrorism operations, humanitarian projects, and training missions, backed by billions of dollars of taxpayer money, have all evaporated in the face of coups, civil wars, human rights abuses, terror attacks, and poorly coordinated aid efforts. The human toll is incalculable. And there appears to be no end in sight.

A Calendar with No Tomorrows

Inside a United Nations office elsewhere in South Sudan, I see a box of almost untouched 2014 calendars. I pick one up and casually flip through it. January offers a photo of two statuesque women modeling locally made clothing and jewelry. February showcases the "first batch of South Sudan National Police Service immigration officers." There's a photo of a woman with a big, warm smile at the Jebel Market in Juba (April) and men working on building a new passenger boat in Malakal (August). The photo for December 2014 shows a young girl skipping rope. The caption reads: "Child enjoying peace in Nyeel, Unity State."

It's quickly clear why the calendars were never put into circulation. In fact, the front cover has this caption: "Building on Peace," while the next page has a grimly farcical quality to it. "Peace and stability in South Sudan," it says, "have allowed Africa's newest nation to turn its attention to development." In the same light, here in South Sudan and across significant parts of the continent, AFRICOM's mission statement reads like satire from the *Onion*. The command, it says in part, promotes "regional security, stability, and prosperity."

Certainly, there's precious little security, stability, or prosperity in Giel's life. Nor does there appear to be any on the horizon for Nyadoang's newborn. The same could be said for so many youths in Ebola-ravaged neighborhoods of Sierra Leone or Liberia, the war-torn Central African Republic, militia-ridden Libya, fragile Somalia, increasingly unstable Kenya, insurgency-racked Mali, or Boko Haram–terrorized Nigeria to name a few of the nations that have received abundant US military attention over the past decade.

As a species, we do a horrible job of predicting the future. But if the past is any guide, US operations will increase in Africa in the years ahead alongside increased insecurity, instability, and strife. Odds are, much of the former will occur below the radar and much of the latter will go unnoticed by most Americans. But make no mistake, for America in the years ahead, Africa will continue to be tomorrow's battlefield.

US Africa Command Debates TomDispatch: An Exchange on the Nature of the US Military Presence in Africa

Soon after publishing my first article on US military efforts in Africa in July 2012, TomDispatch's editor in chief, Tom Engelhardt, received a detailed response from Colonel Tom Davis of AFRICOM's Office of Public Affairs refuting my article point by point. I replied with a detailed rebuttal of each of Davis's contentions and both letters were published in their entirety at TomDispatch on July 26, 2012, allowing readers to draw their own conclusions on the merits of our arguments. A day later, AFRICOM posted Davis's letter on its official website, where it remains as of this writing in late 2014. The command never extended the same courtesy by posting my response. That fact and the exceptionally defensive nature of Davis's letter all but assured me AFRICOM had something to hide and spurred my efforts to continue reporting on American military operations in Africa.

In my letter to Davis, I requested basic information on US military activities. More than two years later, after many follow-up phone and email conversations and messages, that information has yet to arrive, despite repeated assurances by various command spokespersons that my questions would be answered. I also requested the opportunity to report from AFRICOM facilities. This has never been granted either. In addition to the public letter below, I followed up with a personal email to Davis, requesting the chance to speak with him directly. A subordinate responded in his stead. In August 2012, that spokesman said Colonel Davis was on leave. As of the writing of this, he has yet to respond.

What follows is our original exchange, posted at TomDispatch on July 26, 2012.

FROM: Colonel Tom Davis
Director, U.S. Africa Command Office of Public Affairs
Kelley Barracks, Stuttgart, Germany
TO: Mr. Tom Engelhardt, Editor

Dear Mr. Engelhardt,

We read the recent article "Secret Wars, Secret Bases, and the Pentagon's 'New Spice Route' in Africa" with great interest. It is clear the author, Nick Turse, conducted a great deal of research, including reaching out to us, and we welcomed the opportunity to highlight U.S. Africa Command's mission and activities. However, there were several inaccuracies and misrepresentations that we would like to address. My hope is that you, through your publication, will correct the record. As a thought provoking, responsible, and professional journalist, I know that you would want to ensure all reporting was based on facts, not innuendos or misperceptions.

Below are the items U.S. Africa Command would like to address:

"They call it the New Spice Route": This was a term used informally by a few of our logistics specialists to describe the intra-theater transportation system, primarily land shipments from Djibouti, which provides logistical support for U.S. military activities in Africa. The network is officially called the AFRICOM Surface Distribution Network. However, to call it a "superpower's superhighway" is very misleading. The U.S. military cargo transported along these different transportation nodes represents only a mere fraction—i.e., a handful of trucks per week intermixed among the thousands of others—of the total amount of fuel, food, and equipment transported along these routes each day.

"Fast-growing U.S. military presence in Africa": While the size of the U.S. military footprint in Africa has increased since the creation of U.S. Africa Command in October 2008, to call it "fast-growing" is an exaggeration. At the end of October 2008, there were about 2,600 U.S. military personnel and Department of Defense civilians on the African continent or on ships within the command's area of responsibility. The number today is about 5,000, more than half of which represents the service members who serve tours at Camp Lemonnier in Djibouti, with the remainder serving on a temporary basis ranging from a few days to a few weeks. Much of this change is attributable to an increase in the number of exercises and military-to-military engagement programs in order to better enable African nations and regional organizations to strengthen their defense capabilities. On a much smaller scale, it also reflects a modest increase in the staff sizes of DOD offices resident in U.S. embassies, which average just a small number of staff members. But even 5,000 personnel—about the military population of a small Air Force Base in the U.S.—spread across an area that covers 54 countries and major portions of two oceans can hardly be called a "scramble for Africa."

In our view, this is very positive, and testament to our desire to be a security partner of choice in Africa. It reflects an increase in military assistance engagement activities—all of which are requested and approved by the host nation. While we work to advance the security interests of the U.S., we are together addressing what are clearly shared security interests.

"The U.S. maintains a surprising number of bases in Africa": This is incorrect. In the lexicon of the U.S. military, the word "base" implies a certain size, level of infrastructure, and permanence. Based on this widely accepted definition, other than our base at Camp Lemonnier in Djibouti, we do not have military bases in Africa, nor do we have plans to establish any. We do, however, have temporary facilities elsewhere in Africa that support much smaller numbers of personnel, usually for a specific activity. In all cases, our personnel are guests within the host-nation and work alongside or coordinate their activities with host-nation personnel. Some of these locations are fairly well developed while others are more austere.

For example, approximately 100 U.S. military advisors are dispersed among four nations in Central and East Africa providing advice and assistance to the national militaries working to end the threat posed by the Lord's Resistance Army (LRA). We currently have small teams in Obo and Djema in the Central African Republic, Dungu in the Democratic Republic of the Congo, Nzara in South Sudan, and Entebbe in Uganda. In each location, we are working alongside the national militaries, helping to reinforce their efforts and strengthen collaboration and coordination, not conducting our own operations.

Similarly, there are humanitarian work sites in Ethiopian

towns such as Humble, Hulla, and Dube, where Seabees and other U.S. military personnel have assisted in the past or are currently assisting with drilling wells, providing medical and veterinary assistance, or constructing schools and health clinics.

Finally, Thebephatswa Airbase in Molepolole, Botswana, is staffed and operated by Botswana Defence Force personnel (BDFP). There is no permanent U.S. presence on the airbase, nor has there ever been. The United States has partnered with Botswana for previous exercises at Thebephatswa Airbase and much of SOUTHERN ACCORD, a major bilateral exercise in August, will be conducted at Thebephatswa.

We also currently have warehousing privileges at Mombasa International Airport in Kenya, which includes the storage of equipment and rations. U.S. personnel do not manage the warehouses; the daily activities and running of the warehouse are handled by local nationals hired by the Embassy and funded by AFRICOM.

"100 to 200 U.S. commandos share a base with the Kenyan military at Manda Bay": This is also incorrect. U.S. military personnel deployed to Manda Bay are primarily Civil Affairs, Seabees, and security personnel involved with military to military engagements with Kenyan forces and humanitarian initiatives. Simba was established in 2004 to provide support to U.S. military engagements with the Kenyan Navy. Its primary mission is to provide base/life support services to U.S. military personnel who are in the area for training and engagement activities with the Kenyan military, including maritime engagement and civil-military efforts.

"The U.S. also has had troops deployed in Mali": To clarify, prior to the coup, the U.S. military had a longstanding military partnership with Mali. For several years, we had small teams regularly travel in and out of Mali for training activities with the

Malian military; this includes conventional forces and special operations forces (SOF).

At the time of the military seizure on March 22, U.S. Africa Command had a small number of personnel in Mali who were supporting our military-to-military activities. Military assistance to Mali was suspended immediately following the seizure. U.S. government personnel from many agencies, including DoD, remained on stand-by in Bamako as negotiations continued toward a return to democratic, constitutional, civilian rule. Because of the continued uncertainty surrounding the outcome and consequences of the seizure, and the fact that military engagement had only been suspended, our personnel remained in Mali to provide assistance to the Embassy, maintain situational awareness on the unfolding events, and assist in coordination between U.S. Africa Command and the Embassy.

The U.S. State Department terminated foreign assistance to the government of Mali on April 10. The Department of Defense's Defense Security Cooperation Agency received a memorandum from the State Department dated 19 April notifying the DoD of the coup designation and the termination of all military assistance programs. Upon receiving this notification from State Department, we began arranging the departure of personnel and equipment from Mali. All U.S. military personnel who were in Mali supporting military-to-military engagement activities have since departed Mali. Only those Department of Defense personnel regularly assigned to the Embassy (such as the Defense Attaché or U.S. Marine Corps guards) remain.

Also, the introduction to the story states it was recently "revealed" that three U.S. soldiers were killed in an accident in Mali in April and that "This is how we know that U.S. special operations forces were operating in chaotic, previously democratic Mali." The fact is we issued a press release a day after the soldiers were killed, and the Associated Press, Xinhua, and AFP ran stories on the incident. It must be noted that the activities of U.S. military forces in Mali have been very public. We have published stories, fact sheets, and photos on our website, and Malian, U.S. and international reporters have covered these activities for some years.

"Additionally, U.S. Special Operations Forces are engaged in missions against the Lord's Resistance Army": While our forces live and work closely with African security forces, our focus is on enabling their ability to better conduct command and control, planning and coordination. Special Operations Forces are not directly involved in the African-led operation to remove the threat of the LRA. The mission for U.S. forces in Uganda, the Democratic Republic of Congo, Central African Republic (CAR), and South Sudan is to advise and assist local forces to better enable them to conduct their operations. As a matter of fact, in April 2012, we organized a four-day press event in Uganda and CAR, providing 18 local and international journalists' access to cover the African-led counter-LRA mission. This visit resulted in extensive worldwide coverage of the story, which clearly articulated our advise and assist mission.

"And that's still just a part of the story": Yes, we've trained Ugandan, Burundian, and Djiboutian troops supporting the African Union Mission in Somalia (AMISOM). As part of the C-LRA media trip mentioned above, we also brought the media to visit the AMISOM train-up efforts—all taking place at a Uganda People's Defense Force base outside Kampala, Uganda. This visit also resulted in extensive worldwide media coverage. We've also trained Senegalese and Rwandan troops supporting the UN Mission in Darfur (UNAMID), as well as peacekeepers from nearly a dozen other African countries. We apply the resources that we do have to help countries willing to contribute to multinational efforts like AMISOM or UNAMID so that they can continue their operations. Our engagement in this realm is in support of a State Department–led peacekeeping training program, which has trained more than 200,000 African peacekeepers from 25 African nations over the years. Recently we've seen positive results in Mogadishu, not only as a result of the U.S. support, but more importantly, because of the brave men and women of the AMISOM troop-contributing nations.

Like every Geographic Combatant Command, we have an exercise program with nations within our area of responsibility. We currently have 14 major bilateral and multilateral exercises that have been conducted or are planned for 2012 and as many in 2013. As you probably know, many security issues in Africa are best addressed multilaterally. Exercises are a critical engagement opportunity that not only allow for improvements to interoperability, but also foster greater regional cooperation and integration.

We also conduct some type of military training or military-to-military engagement or activity with nearly every country on the African continent. This is part of our effort to enable African nations to increase their defense capabilities. These activities are requested by the host nation and cleared by the U.S. embassies. Many are well covered by local press and highlighted on our website.

"Next year, even more American troops are likely to be on hand": The 2nd Brigade Combat Team, 1st Infantry Division will not deploy to Africa. Instead, the brigade acts as a single source to provide U.S. Army personnel to support activities already tasked to our Army service component, U.S. Army Africa. Previously, the requirements were distributed across the entire U.S. Army. Under this new construct, these same requirements will be filled from a single unit allowing personnel from this brigade to establish a level of expertise on the African continent. This change will not increase the number of Soldiers on the continent, but simplifies our internal processes for identifying Soldiers to support existing missions.

We must note that reports that leap to the conclusion that "3,000 Soldiers will deploy to Africa" are inaccurate. Small teams—whose numbers typically range from 3–12—would be drawn from this unit to conduct deliberately planned engagements, training events, and exercises. Once or twice a year, to support a large-scale exercise, they may send a few hundred. This process is evolving. But, when their missions are complete, they return home. This can be compared to the SPMAGTF-12 cited in the article, whose Marines are not only doing great work for Uganda and Burundi and other partner nations, but also America, Americans, and American interests.

"Mercenary cargo carriers to skirt diplomatic clearance issues": The choice of words is interesting and unfortunate. This is only one example where somewhat inflammatory language is used to make a point but at the expense of the credibility of the report. What exactly is a mercenary cargo carrier? Federal Express, DHL, Ethiopian Air, and other reputable air cargo companies we use to transport material? The choice to use contract carriers is based exclusively on cost and efficiency. And, to be very clear, we are always required to obtain diplomatic clearance and complete all customs formalities. It would be highly inappropriate and unethical to attempt to "skirt" country clearances. To do that would be an egregious violation of our values. In fact, since these actions appear to constitute criminal activity, we would be appreciative if Mr. Turse can provide us specific details, documents, or other evidence, in order to provide our Criminal Investigative Command (CID) a basis of information to start an investigation. To be perfectly clear, AFRICOM does not condone this type of behavior, anything you can do to provide us the needed evidence would be appreciated.

"Emergency Troop Housing": All of the military construction projects you outline are included in the Defense Authorization Acts of FY 2010 and 2011 and are a matter of public record. However, the 300 additional Containerized Living Units (CLUs) are being built for people already living at Camp Lemonnier, either in tents or in other substandard housing, not for new arrivals.

We appreciate Mr. Turse contacting us for information and running our input in the final article. He followed up with us with a list of questions that required much more time than the one business day he gave us to answer. It took several days to conduct the research necessary to answer his questions; unfortunately, he chose to publish the story prior to receiving the answers, which he knew we were working on. If he had waited, we would have provided the information requested, which could have better informed his story. It takes time to gather information about locations in seven different countries.

Finally, I would encourage you and those who have interest in what we do to review our Website, www.AFRICOM.mil, and a new Defense Department Special Web Report on U.S. Africa Command at this link http://www.defense.gov/home/features/2012/0712_AFRICOM/.

Please do not hesitate to contact us in the future if you have any questions or need any additional information.

Sincerely,
Tom Davis,
Colonel, U.S. Army
Director of Public Affairs
United States Africa Command

Nick Turse's Response

From: Nick Turse

To: Tom Davis

Dear Colonel Davis,

Thank you very much for your note. It's flattering that you and your colleagues read my article, "Obama's Scramble for Africa: Secret Wars, Secret Bases, and the Pentagon's 'New Spice Route' in Africa," with such interest. It's always gratifying to know that a piece has had an impact on readers.

I appreciate your regard for the "great deal of research" that I conducted and am grateful for the information that your command released to me. I do, however, object to your assertion that the article contained "several inaccuracies and misrepresentations." Most of your "refutations" actually seem to corroborate my assertions and I believe that, by and large, your objections have largely to do with semantics and differences of interpretation. But let me respond, point by point:

"They call it the New Spice Route": I'm glad to have you confirm this fact. I do, however, find it odd that you refer to this as an informal term, since this is how the supply network was referred to in an official military publication (*Army Sustainment*). In fact, the article by Lieutenant Colonel David Corrick was even titled "The New Spice Route for Africa." To describe it as consisting of "primarily land shipments from Djibouti" also seems to run counter to the information in Lieutenant Colonel Corrick's article. A map of "The New Spice Route" that appeared with his article indicates that the supply network consists of land and sea routes linking Mombasa, Kenya, and Manda Bay, Kenya; Mombasa and Garissa, Kenya; Mombasa and Nairobi, Kenya; Nairobi and Entebbe, Uganda; Mombasa and a Djiboutian port; and a

Djiboutian port with Dire Dawa, Ethiopia. To complain about my calling it a "superpower's superhighway," on the basis of the total percentage of cargo that travels along the route, strikes me as nitpicking over a difference of interpretation.

Quite obviously, this is not how you would characterize it and I respect that. I see the matter differently, however. The United States is still a superpower—on this, I suspect, we would both agree—and this is the network by which it speeds food, fuel, and equipment to keep its operations in Africa running. I would also hasten to add that military personnel associated with the program characterize it not as some second-rate Djiboutian trucking effort, but as "innovative," "high-tech," and "transformational." This is their language, not mine. Moreover, Lieutenant Colonel Corrick writes that the network is growing and that it "will eventually span all of Africa."

"Fast-growing U.S. military presence in Africa": You question this phrasing in my piece. Once again, your complaint about inaccuracy seems to me to be based on what is, at best, a matter of opinion—although I obviously believe that the facts demonstrate otherwise. To base the bulk of your contentions strictly on troop-level increases strikes me as a very limited way of assessing growth. The US military "presence" anywhere is much more that simply a question of troop levels. (Nevertheless, given that the US is technically not "at war" in Africa, the more than 200 percent increase in US personnel there since 2005 seems striking to me.)

Back in 2003, the US military hardly had a foothold in Africa. Today, there is a major base in Djibouti (now slated for many improvements and expansion), contingents of US personnel have been deployed to the Central African Republic, Democratic Republic of Congo, Ethiopia, Kenya, Mali, South Sudan, and the Seychelles Islands; troops have conducted operations in Burundi, Liberia, Somalia, and Uganda. Then there's that expanding supply network I wrote about. There's also the growing Tusker Sand program of aerial surveillance missions that the *Washington Post* exposed. You even state that AFRICOM conducts "some type of military training or military-to-military engagement or activity with nearly every country on the African continent." The list goes on and on. I stand by this assessment and consider it well documented.

"The U.S. maintains a surprising number of bases in Africa": You deny that the places I identified are "bases." I understand that you don't label them as such, but that doesn't mean others don't. Let me start by noting this: I was more than fair in making certain that readers knew AFRICOM and I differed in our interpretations. At the beginning of my article, I explicitly noted: "According to Pat Barnes, a spokesman for U.S. Africa Command (AFRICOM), Camp Lemonnier serves as the only official U.S. base on the continent."

Shortly thereafter, I again drew attention to this distinction, and our differing interpretations of what constitutes a base, when I wrote: "Today—official designations aside—the U.S. maintains a surprising number of bases in Africa." Neither you personally nor the US military are the ultimate arbiters of what constitutes a base. You have your own definition, nothing more. *Webster's* begins its relevant entry on "base" as "the place from which a military force draws supplies." That seems to encompass a good many facilities along that "New Spice Route" in Africa. But resorting to dictionaries, either yours or *Webster's*, seems beside the point. When the *Washington Post* first wrote about US operations in Obo in the Central African Republic, it began its article this way: "Behind razor wire and bamboo walls topped with security cameras sits one of the newest U.S. military outposts in Africa. U.S. Special Forces soldiers with tattooed forearms and sunglasses emerge daily in pickup trucks that carry weapons, supplies and interpreters." Whether you call that an "outpost," a "base," or a "camp" matters little. It is clearly a protected compound that houses military personnel, supplies, and equipment. If it looks like a duck and it quacks like a duck . . .

Additionally, your letter could be read to imply that I claim the United States had outposts at Thebephatswa Airbase in Molepolole, Botswana, or Mombasa International Airport in Kenya. To be clear, I never wrote any such thing. I asked your command for comment for my article about these and other sites, but none was offered until your note, which arrived more than a week after the article was published. As such, I did not publish anything about these facilities. It seems that, just as I suspected, they have been or are currently integral to the US military project in Africa, so I appreciate the information.

You will note that, in regard to Camp Gilbert in Dire Dawa, Ethiopia, and a Navy port facility in Djibouti, I specifically mentioned in my article that "AFRICOM did not respond to requests for further information on these posts before this article went to press." To this day, no one has responded to my requests for information about these possible bases. What should I make of this pregnant silence?

"100 to 200 U.S. commandos share a base with the Kenyan military at Manda Bay": You will need to take this up with the *Washington Post*. The sentence, in full, reads: "A recent investigation by the *Washington Post* revealed that contractor-operated surveillance aircraft based out of Entebbe, Uganda, are scouring the territory used by Kony's LRA at the Pentagon's behest, and that 100 to 200 U.S. commandos share a base with the Kenyan military at Manda Bay." Specifically, the *Washington Post* states: "Manda Bay, Kenya: More than 100 U.S. commandos are based at a Kenyan military installation."

To be clear, I did not want to rely on the *Washington Post*'s reporting, but was left with no choice. Ten days before my article was published, I specifically asked your spokesman about the troops stationed at Manda Bay as well as the nature of the operations there, but my questions were never answered. I asked in a slightly different manner six days before publication, but again received no answer. Your letter to my editor, more than a week after publication, was the first response I received on the subject from AFRICOM.

"The U.S. also has had troops deployed in Mali": It seems that we are in total agreement that this statement is true.

"Additionally, U.S. Special Operations Forces are engaged in missions against the Lord's Resistance Army": We seem to be in agreement on this as well. I wrote nothing about tactical operations, gun battles, or anything of the sort. In fact, I even quote an AFRICOM spokesman who said, "U.S. military personnel working with regional militaries in the hunt for Joseph Kony are guests of the African security forces comprising the regional counter-LRA effort." I don't know how much clearer I could have been about that. What is very clear is that US troops are thoroughly engaged in missions against the LRA. As an article by the Pentagon's American Forces Press Service explicitly noted: "U.S. troops are providing information- and intelligence-sharing, logistics, communications and other enabling capabilities for host-nation troops pursuing Kony in Uganda, the Central African Republic, South Sudan and the Republic of the Congo."

"And that's still just a part of the story": Given that, in your letter, you chronicle missions above and beyond those that I exposed, I'd say we agree on this point as well.

"Next year, even more American troops are likely to be on hand": You begin by stating, "The 2nd Brigade Combat Team,

1st Infantry Division will not deploy to Africa." I never said otherwise, only—and very specifically—that elements of this BCT would deploy. I never spoke of the full contingent, only units from it. As far as the numbers go, I apologize if these are incorrect. They are, however, publicly reported figures to which I explicitly provided a link as a form of citation. That article, in *Army Times*, is titled: "3,000 soldiers to serve in Africa next year."

Once again, I did not want to have to use figures from a third party in assessing the size of the American contingent in Africa. In fact, I asked the AFRICOM spokesman at the Pentagon, in an email dated July 6, whether the US military presence (which he had already told me was approximately 5,000 at this moment) would grow, shrink, or stay about the same next year, but he never offered an answer. Nor did AFRICOM personnel at your headquarters, to whom he assured me that he passed along my questions, respond. In fact, weeks later, they still have not responded.

"Mercenary cargo carriers to skirt diplomatic clearance issues": You object to my language once again, but don't actually refute the facts. You ask: "What exactly is a mercenary cargo carrier?" I submit that it's a person or company which supports military cargo operations for financial gain. The air carriers you mention are, indeed, military contractors which are supporting military operations for profit, largely unbeknownst to the American public. I firmly stand by this characterization.

You go on to write: "We are always required to obtain diplomatic clearance and complete all customs formalities. It would be highly inappropriate and unethical to attempt to 'skirt' country clearances. To do that would be an egregious violation of our values. In fact, since these actions appear to constitute criminal activity, we would be appreciative if Mr. Turse can provide us specific details, documents, or other evidence, in order to provide our Criminal Investigative Command (CID) a basis of information to start an investigation." To begin, I would refer CID to Major Joseph D. Gaddis of the U.S. Air Force for further information. In a section of an *Army Sustainment* article on air logistics in Africa, titled "The Diplomatic Clearance Hurdle," Major Gaddis writes:

> A major question facing logisticians in Africa is whether the legwork of contracting airlift outweighs the challenges often associated with traditional methods of using U.S. military aircraft in Africa, which include lengthy processes to obtain diplomatic clearance. Carrying out a mission into most countries often requires 14 to 21 days of leadtime. For the Hungary based C–17 unit, this process can be as long as 30 to 45 days. When working with operations in landlocked countries, diplomatic over-flight clearance leadtimes reduce the flexibility of the DOD airlift system. Domestically registered contract aircraft do not have these clearance issues. Their simple country clearance process enables them to plan a flight in less than a day. Foreign civilian carriers operating in Africa (including U.S.-registered carriers) also face less diplomatic red tape and do not require the same lengthy clearance process as the U.S. military.

Gaddis very clearly states: "Domestically registered contract aircraft do not have th[e] clearance issues" that affect US military aircraft. He states explicitly that the United States can skirt lengthy authorization issues by using "Foreign civilian carriers operating in Africa . . . [which] face less diplomatic red tape and do not require the same lengthy clearance process as the U.S. military." This suggests that the United States is making a conscious decision to shift from traditional and more overt methods of shipping equipment and supplies to more covert methods in

order to subvert regulations put in place by African countries—
or at the very least subvert the spirit of those regulations. While
cutting "red tape" appears to be the primary reason for hiding
behind contractors, I can't help but see similarities between this
effort and the use of generic-looking spy planes as part of Tusker
Sand surveillance missions in Africa.

In any case, I would appreciate it if you would keep me ap-
prised of any investigations or other actions that result from this
information.

"Emergency Troop Housing": Again, we seem to be in total agreement that the United States is constructing "Emergency
Troop Housing" in Djibouti. You note that "the 300 additional
Containerized Living Units (CLUs) are being built for people already living at Camp Lemonnier, either in tents or in other substandard housing, not for new arrivals." I just want to make clear
that I never said these CLUs were for "new arrivals." It does, however, make me wonder about why that word "emergency" is being
used for this new housing. I also question why—since you dispute that the US presence in Africa is fast-growing—troops have
been living in substandard housing? If there was no rush and you
have plenty of time to plan for arrivals, why wasn't adequate troop
housing constructed in advance?

Finally, I respectfully take issue with your comments about
my requests to AFRICOM for information for my article, which
was published on July 12, 2012. As your records will attest, on
May 29, 2012, I first asked for detailed information on the US
military presence in Africa, specifically bases—including those at
which US troops are guests of other nations. On June 6, I received
a rather superficial reply to which I followed up with questions,
by phone or email—sometimes both—on July 2, 6, and 9. I even
followed up after the story was published and was told I would be

contacted with answers by Wednesday, July 16, by a specific individual at AFRICOM. At this writing, on July 24, I am still waiting to hear from him.

I also object to your claim that I "followed up . . . with a list of questions that required much more time than the one business day he gave us to answer." To be frank, in my "business" there are no "business days." And let's be franker still: there aren't any in yours, either. Other than holiday ceasefires and the like, I've never heard about the US military taking a week off from a war or shutting down for the weekend. My work adheres to the same schedule.

Still, the list of questions to which you refer was first called in to your Pentagon spokesman on July 6. He asked me to put them in writing, which I dutifully did. I sent those in and he assured me that he forwarded them on to your headquarters that same day. I followed up on the 9th and mentioned my looming deadline. I was told that AFRICOM headquarters might have some answers for me on the 10th. That day, however, came and went without a word. So did the 11th. We published the piece on the 12th.

Given that I've been requesting detailed information since May, I'm sorry to say that your letter rings a bit hollow when you write: "If he had waited, we would have provided the information requested, which could have better informed his story." Two weeks later, I'm still waiting for a complete reply to my questions of July 6 (not to mention those of May 29). I respectfully submit that a vigorous free press cannot be held hostage, waiting for information that might never arrive.

Quite obviously, we have different worldviews and differing opinions, but to say that my reporting contained several "inaccuracies and misrepresentations" is, I believe, a misrepresentation and I hope you will reconsider your words in light of my response above.

I believe that I was fair in my reporting. I gave ample space to AFRICOM's views and contentions when they differed from mine, provided reasonable-sized quotes so that your spokesman was able to express AFRICOM's opinions, and drew on respected mainstream publications for information when your command did not answer my questions. I would also submit that my reporting gives much greater voice to dissenting views than do the news articles/releases on the AFRICOM website. I gave your spokesman's view on what constitutes a "base." I would challenge your staff to do the same and grant, in news releases and responses to queries, that while the US military might not consider a facility to be a "base," others could have a different opinion.

Moreover, let me suggest that if AFRICOM were entirely transparent—and posting reams of information to your website is not the same as transparency—with America's taxpayers about US military operations in Africa, all of this could be avoided.

With this and future articles on US operations in Africa in mind, let me ask (with plenty of time to spare) for a full listing of all—as you term them—"temporary facilities" and any other sites where the United States has or has had "warehousing privileges," construction projects, work sites, outposts, camps, facilities, laboratories, warehouses, supply depots, fuel storage, and the like in Africa since 2003, as well as supporting documents on the nature of the operations at these locations so that I can evaluate them for myself. If I had a clearer picture, I would certainly be in a better position to ask even more informed questions. Once that picture becomes clearer, I would hope that you would facilitate visits by me to these facilities for a firsthand look, so I could draw my own conclusions about their nature.

In addition to providing me with this information, I also

hope you'll allow me to call on you directly the next time I have questions about US operations in Africa.

Thank you again for your interest in my work and for the information your command provided to me.

Regards,
Nick Turse
Associate Editor, TomDispatch.com

Acknowledgments

My name may be the one on the cover, but books—especially investigative efforts like this one—are a collective endeavor. As always, I relied on the support of family, friends, and colleagues and stood on the shoulders of other journalists whose intrepid work helped make mine possible. For all those I'm unable to mention here, I offer a collective round of thank-yous.

I also want to express my deep and sincere gratitude to Patrick Lannan and Lannan Foundation who not only supported my work at TomDispatch and provided the assistance that launched my writings on Africa, but also provided me the unforgettable opportunity to think and write in Marfa, Texas. For the latter, I also extend thanks to Martha Jessup and Douglas Humble. Memories of that residency will last a lifetime, and some of the fruits of my stay in Marfa reside in this book.

Taya Kitman and everyone at the Nation Institute provided crucial support as well as an intellectual home for me. Andy Breslau stood behind me when US Africa Command attempted to impugn my reporting. Esther Kaplan, Joe Conason, and Sarah Blustain of the Institute's iFund provided critical assistance and helped send me to Africa and to an important conference in

Washington, DC. This travel led directly to four chapters and the afterword of this book. Adelaide Gomer's generosity also supported these trips—to Tanzania, South Sudan, and the National Defense University—enabling me to observe, up close and personal, and better understand the results of US efforts in Africa. They all have my enduring gratitude.

My editor and friend Tom Engelhardt of TomDispatch contributed to each and every one of these chapters by offering always sharp insights, critiques, and the extraordinary editing that has made him famous among writers in the know. My TomDispatch colleagues Andy Kroll, Erika Eichelberger, Christopher Holmes, and Joe Duax all played roles in making chapters of this book better than they would have otherwise been and have my deep thanks.

What luck I've had to begin working with Anthony Arnove in these last years. Impresario, dynamo, and maybe the best-connected man on the Southpaw side of the spectrum, it was Anthony who came up with the idea of this book, and it isn't the first time his vision was of immense benefit to me. Many thanks also go to the entire crew at Haymarket Books who provide a home for the Dispatch Books imprint and create paperback gems, like this one, that help print hold the line in the digital age.

Roane Carey of the *Nation* was instrumental in facilitating the reporting in this book. Annelise Whitley of the Nation Institute helped make it possible for me to squeeze limited but crucial tidbits of information out of US Africa Command. While the US government wasn't terribly helpful in facilitating my work—obstructing my efforts in innumerable ways and taking opacity to new levels—I'm grateful for the efforts of individuals whose work lived up to the spirit of transparency promised by the Obama White House, especially the staff of the FOIA office at US Army

Africa. Thanks also to US military photographers whose images I use in this book as well as the men and women of the Government Accountability Office and the Pentagon's Office of the Inspector General for their important work and their assistance to me, personally. AFRICOM Public Affairs office claims that it "fulfills the command's obligation to keep . . . the American people and the international community informed of its activities." I've seen little evidence of that. But I am grateful whenever they deign to respond to my questions, and my fingers remain crossed that they'll eventually live up to their mission statement and allow me a firsthand look at their operations one day.

Many people helped make my reporting in South Sudan possible. I especially want to thank Shantal Persaud of the United Nations Mission in South Sudan for getting me to and from Malakal—a none-too-simple feat—and Eshe Hussein for her assistance once I arrived there. I also want to thank all the representatives of NGOs who took the time to talk with me, on and off the record, and especially all the South Sudanese willing to speak with a stranger about the sad state of their new nation. Back in the United States, David Rosner and Kathy Conway smoothed the way for my trip more than they'll ever know. Dana Blaney did me a huge favor and will always have my thanks.

Most of all, I want to thank Tam, the true light of my life, for making all my work possible and inspiring me every day. Without her, my reporting in Africa would have been impossible; without her, this book would not exist; without her, I would be lost. There is not space enough to express my gratitude or my love.

A Note on the Text

The pieces that make up *Tomorrow's Battlefield* were written between July 2012 and November 2014, most of them appearing at TomDispatch.com. To assemble this book, they were edited, sometimes updated, and mostly trimmed of the telltale signs of the immediate moment—all those "recentlys" and "last months"—along with the sorts of repetitions that are natural in pieces written successively and all focused on the same large topic. Otherwise the articles are reproduced as they first appeared with only two significant changes. Online, they bristle with links to source material. I encourage those interested in delving further into the subjects covered in this book to visit the original articles at TomDispatch and explore those citations. In addition, if you want to see the black-and-white maps, briefing slides, and photographs in this book in full color, consult their online versions as well.

Index

About Nick Turse

Nick Turse is an award-winning journalist, historian, essayist, the managing editor of TomDispatch.com and a fellow at the Nation Institute. He is the cofounder and coeditor in chief of Dispatch Books, the author of *The Complex: How the Military Invades Our Everyday Lives* (Metropolitan Books, 2008), the editor of *The Case for Withdrawal from Afghanistan* (Verso, 2010), and the coauthor of *Terminator Planet: The First History of Drone Warfare, 2001–2050* (Dispatch Books, 2012). His *Kill Anything That Moves: The Real American War in Vietnam* was published by Metropolitan Books in 2013.

A national security reporter and historian of the Vietnam War, Turse has written for the *Los Angeles Times*, *San Francisco Chronicle*, the *Nation*, *Adbusters*, *GOOD*, *Le Monde Diplomatique*, *In These Times*, *Mother Jones*, and the *Village Voice*, among other print and online publications.

Turse, who holds a PhD in sociomedical sciences from Columbia University, was the recipient of a Ridenhour Prize for Investigative Reporting at the National Press Club in April 2009 and a James Aronson Award for Social Justice Journalism from Hunter College. He has previously been awarded a Guggenheim fellowship as well as fellowships at New York University's Center for the United States and the Cold War and Harvard University's Radcliffe Institute for Advanced Study. He has also received grants from the Fund for Investigative Journalism and the Pulitzer Center for Crisis Reporting.

He is married to Tam Turse, a photographer with whom he has collaborated on several reporting projects.

About TomDispatch

Tom Engelhardt launched TomDispatch.com in October 2001 as an email publication offering commentary and collected articles from the world press. In December 2002, it gained its name, became a project of the Nation Institute, and went online as "a regular antidote to the mainstream media." The site now features three articles a week, all original. These include Engelhardt's regular commentaries as well as the work of authors ranging from Rebecca Solnit, Bill McKibben, Andrew Bacevich, Barbara Ehrenreich, and Mike Davis to Michael Klare, Adam Hochschild, Noam Chomsky, and Karen J. Greenberg. Nick Turse, who also writes for the site, is its managing editor. Andy Kroll is its associate editor and economic correspondent. Timothy MacBain produces regular TomCast audio interviews with TomDispatch authors, and Erika Eichelberger handles the site's social media. Christopher Holmes is its eagle-eyed proofreader. TomDispatch is intended to introduce readers to voices and perspectives from elsewhere (even when that elsewhere is here). Its mission is to connect some of the global dots regularly left unconnected by the mainstream media and to offer a clearer sense of how this imperial globe of ours actually works.

About Dispatch Books

As an editor at Pantheon Books in the 1970s and 1980s, Tom Engelhardt used to jokingly call himself publishing's "editor of last resort." His urge to rescue books and authors rejected elsewhere brought the world Eduardo Galeano's beautiful *Memory of Fire* trilogy and Art Spiegelman's Pulitzer Prize–winning *Maus*, among other notable, incendiary, and worthy works. In that spirit, he and award-winning journalist Nick Turse founded Dispatch Books, a publishing effort offering a home to authors used to operating outside the mainstream.

With an eye for well-crafted essays, illuminating long-form investigative journalism, and compelling subjects given short shrift by the big publishing houses, Engelhardt and Turse seek to provide readers with electronic and print books of conspicuous quality offering unique perspectives found nowhere else. In a world in which publishing giants take fewer and fewer risks and style regularly trumps substance, Dispatch Books aims to be the informed reader's last refuge for uncommon voices, new perspectives, and provocative critiques.

Dispatch Books' first effort, *Terminator Planet*, explored the military's increasing use of remotely piloted drones, which have turned visions of a dystopian future into an increasingly dystopian present. Now teamed with Haymarket Books, one of the leading progressive publishers in the United States, Dispatch Books exposes and analyzes the new model of US warfare with *The Changing Face of Empire*.